Reader's Digest
Home
Decorating
Manual

18123908

Expert guidance on practical decorating tasks for the home

Published by
The Reader's Digest Association Limited
London • New York • Sydney • Montreal

Contents

Wallpapering

Tiling

Floors

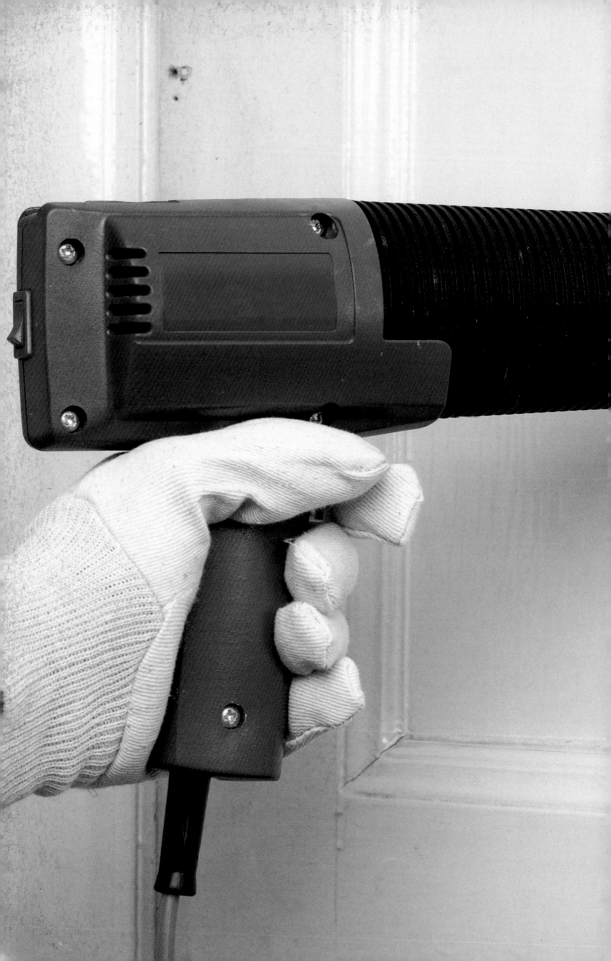

Preparation

Tools for preparation

A huge variety of tools is available, and new ones are being introduced all the time. Choosing the right tools can make a job both faster and easier.

Sanding tools Have a variety of abrasive papers to hand for smoothing filler or any roughness on stripped walls or woodwork. Wet-and-dry paper can be used dry or damped with water. A flexible sanding block has an abrasive coating on four sides. Rinse and squeeze out before using to rub down a painted surface, destroying the glaze and removing dirt before repainting. Powered sanding tools clean stripped surfaces quickly. But don't try to strip paint with a sander as the abrasive will become clogged.

Heavy-duty scraper with replaceable blades

Scrapers/strippers Scrapers or stripping knives have a flat, slightly sprung blade. Broad scrapers (opposite) are used for stripping wallpaper. Some have a long handle for leverage and strong, sharp replaceable blades (above). Narrow scrapers and shave hooks, with triangular or curved blades set at right angles to the handle (opposite), are used to remove softened paint from flat and moulded woodwork.

Flexible sanding block

Wire brush Used to remove loose or flaking material; available as a hand tool or as a fitting for an electric drill.

Protect yourself Each year many injuries are caused by rust particles or tile chips flying into eyes or burns from paint-stripping chemicals. Wear safety goggles to protect your eyes; wear a face mask if there is a lot of dust; protect your hands with suitable gloves; keep dirt out of your hair with a cap or scarf; and put on ear defenders for noisy jobs.

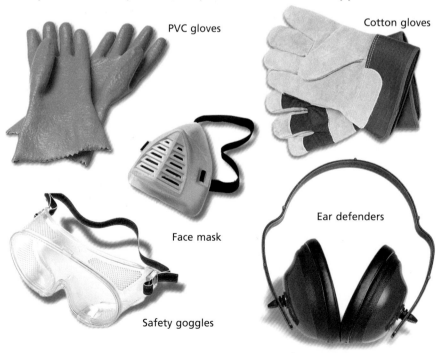

PVC gloves

Cotton gloves

Ear defenders

Face mask

Safety goggles

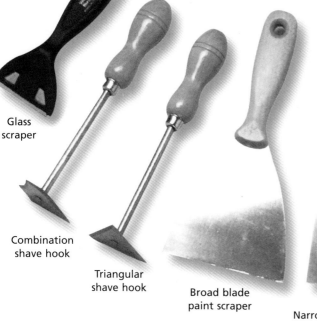

Glass
scraper

Combination
shave hook

Triangular
shave hook

Broad blade
paint scraper

Narrow blade
paint scraper

Broad blade
filling knife

Narrow blade
filling knife

Filling knife A filling knife is like a scraper with a more flexible blade. Use it to press filler into holes and cracks and to level it flush with the surface.

Hot-air guns Hot-air guns have largely superseded blowtorches to soften paint before stripping. They work like a superheated hair dryer and are much safer than blowtorches as there is no naked flame.

Hot-air gun

Steam stripper This is the most efficient tool for stripping washable wallpaper or papered surfaces that have been painted. It consists of a water reservoir and a hose, which is connected to a steam plate. When the water heats up, steam is forced up the hose and out through the plate. This penetrates the wall covering and softens the adhesive underneath (painted paper must first be scored). Steam strippers can be hired, but it may be worth buying one if you plan to strip more than one room.

Preparing walls and ceilings

Any professional decorator will tell you that preparation is crucial to a good finish. It's time-consuming and hard work stripping off old finishes – and even new, bare plaster needs priming – but your job will be far easier if you know what to do.

Painted surfaces

Gloss painted
• If repainting and existing paint is sound, wash with sugar soap and water.
• If papering, rub surface with a damp flexible sanding pad to remove the sheen and provide a key. Ideally, hang lining paper.

Emulsion painted
• If emulsion is peeling, strip back to a sound base. There may be distemper underneath.
• If the emulsion is sound, wash and roughen the surface with sugar soap and water.
• If papering, use heavy-duty paste with minimum water.

Distemper
Distemper forms a chalky barrier, preventing paint or paper adhering to the wall.
• Scrub off with a rough cloth or a nylon pan scourer and water.
• If there is a thick coating, damp the whole area, then scrape with a wide stripping knife. Never scrape bad cases of distemper without wetting it; it makes too much mess.
• Coat any remaining distemper with stabilising solution and leave to dry.

Wallpapered surfaces

Standard wallpaper
• Soften ordinary wallpaper with water and a little washing-up liquid.
• Add a handful of cellulose paste to each bucket of water – it helps to hold the water on the wall.
• Use a scraper to lift off the paper.

Painted wallpaper
• Roughen the surface with coarse abrasive paper before you wet it or use a steamer.

• If the paint is thick, you may have to score the surface with a wallpaper scorer.
• Never use a wire brush – if slivers of metal become embedded in the plaster, they will rust and stain wall coverings.

Washable and vinyl papers
• Buy or hire a steam wallpaper stripper especially if the wall is covered with layers of old paper. Score the surface first so that water can penetrate.
• Vinyls are easier to strip – the vinyl skin can be pulled from its backing, then the backing can be soaked and stripped.
• With some modern papers and vinyls (called easy strip), the backing can be left on the wall as lining paper for the next wallcovering. This only works if the paper is firmly stuck to the wall. If there are any loose areas, strip the whole lot off.

Tiles, textures and bricks

Imitation tiling
This looks a bit like vinyl flooring on the wall. It was usually put up with a strong adhesive and can be hard to remove.
• Pull the top layer from its backing.
• Soak off the backing and old adhesive with hot water, scraping it away as it softens.
• Alternatively, try using a steam wallpaper stripper.
• If the adhesive is very stubborn, try using a hot-air gun to soften it.

Polystyrene tiles
Expanded polystyrene ceiling tiles can be painted with emulsion but never with gloss paint. To remove tiles, lever each one away from the surface and then scrape off the glue (see page 18).

LEAD IN PAINT

Paint with a high lead content can cause lead poisoning. All household paint in the UK is now completely lead-free. However, paint in older houses – as a rough benchmark, pre-1960s – may contain lead. Use a Lead Paint Test Kit to check. If the surface is sound, paint over it. If you need to strip the paint, take precautions: always wear a face mask conforming to BS EN149 and open the windows to ensure good ventilation. Use a liquid chemical stripper, put all waste into a sealed bag and consult your local Environmental Health Department for details of safe disposal.

Ceramic tiles

If tiles are to be painted, make sure they are clean and dry, then use a specialist tile paint. You cannot hang wallpaper over tiles so you may wish to remove them (page 18). This is hard work, and afterwards you may need to replaster the wall.

Cork tiles

Cork tiles cannot be painted over, though you may be able to cover them with lining paper and wallpaper.
• Prise each tile away from the wall with a wide stripping knife or a bolster chisel.
• To remove hard lumps of glue, follow the instructions for taking down expanded polystyrene tiles on page 18.

Textured coatings

Thick coatings applied by brush or roller on ceilings and walls are difficult to remove.
• You could try using a steam stripper.
• Alternatively, try a proprietary textured-paint remover which works like a chemical paint stripper.
• If you simply want to repaint the textured surface, lightly scrub it with a mild solution of sugar soap and water and allow to dry.

Exposed brick

• Brush the bricks to remove dust.
• Paint interior bricks with emulsion or leave unpainted.

Steam-stripping a ceiling

You can use a steam wallpaper stripper to remove old painted or washable wallpaper from a ceiling. Because you will be using the steaming plate above head level, take precautions to protect yourself from being splashed by very hot water. Wear a baseball cap or similar headgear, safety goggles, a long-sleeved shirt and work gloves. Set up a work platform across the room, rather than trying to work from steps, so you can hold the steaming plate in front of you as you work across the ceiling strip by strip. Put down plenty of dustsheets, and let the scrapings fall to the floor.

A steam stripper will also help to remove old textured ceiling finishes such as Artex, allowing you to scrape the softened coating off area by area. Be warned, however; this is a messy and time-consuming job, and you may prefer to employ a plasterer to apply a skim coat of plaster over the old finish to create a smooth ceiling surface.

Protect light fittings

Use plastic bags to guard ceiling lights and fans against paint drips. First, switch off at the mains, then unscrew the ceiling rose cover and slide it down the flex. Enclose the whole fitting in a bag, securing the neck around the flex with a freezer bag tie. Make tubes from stiff paper to slip over wall lights, removing shades and bulbs first.

Problem surfaces

Efflorescence

Damp can cause chemicals in mortar or plaster to come to the surface and form a whitish fluff called efflorescence. Brush this off the wall, then apply an alkali-resisting primer or a stabilising solution.

Stains

Cover stains caused by plumbing leaks or cigarette tar with an aluminium primer-sealer or an aerosol stain blocker. This will stop the stain from bleeding through the new paint.

Damp

Do not isolate damp by applying an impervious coating – this will simply cause it to move elsewhere, creating fresh problems. Find and cure the cause.

Holes and cracks

Brush away any loose or crumbling plaster from small holes and cracks, and repair the area with an appropriate filler (page 19).

Larger holes, gaps and cracks require more extensive treatment (pages 20–21).

Uneven plaster

Level out slight irregularities with a skimming coat of surface plaster.

Stripping wallpaper

Stripping wallpaper cannot be rushed. If the paper is not wet enough, it will be difficult to remove. Use a scraper and water or a steam stripper, but perforate the paper first so that the water or steam can penetrate the surface and soften the paste.

Tools Bucket; sponge or old paintbrush; dust sheets; wide stripping knife; wallpaper scorer (serrated scraper or orbital scorer).

Materials Water; wallpaper paste; washing-up liquid.

Stripping standard wallpaper

1 Lay down dustsheets then go over the surface of the paper with a scoring tool.

2 Fill a bucket with warm water. Add a handful of wallpaper paste and a squirt of washing-up liquid. The paste helps to hold the water on the wall and the detergent acts as a wetting agent which speeds up the penetration of the water.

3 Apply water generously to a whole wall with a large sponge or an old paintbrush. Leave the water to soak into the surface for at least five minutes.

4 Test to see whether the paper is ready to be stripped. Slide the edge of a wide stripping knife under the wet paper either at the bottom of the length or at a seam.

5 Hold the knife at an angle of about 30° and push it away from you, up the wall. Do not let the blade gouge the plaster. If the paper does not wrinkle and is hard to lift, it needs to soak for longer.

HELPFUL TIP

Wetting the wall with a hand-held garden spray gun is quicker than using a brush or sponge.

---

6 Sponge on more water if necessary and try the test again – if the paper wrinkles, pull it away from the wall upwards. It should come away in a fairly big strip.

7 Ease the stripper under the wet covering again and continue to peel away paper. If the paper won't come off the wall despite a good soaking, use a steam wallpaper stripper.

TEXTURED WALL COATINGS

Removing a thick textured coating is a messy job – especially if it's on a ceiling. You can use a textured-paint remover or a steam wallpaper stripper. Before you start, clear all furniture and protect the floor with polythene dustsheets and newspaper.

Removing the coating
• If using paint remover, apply thickly with a large paintbrush and leave it to penetrate for the time given on the container. When the surface has softened, strip it off with a wide-bladed wallpaper scraper. Wash the surface with water and washing-up liquid before redecorating.
• If using a steam wallpaper stripper, allow the steam to break through the paint barrier and soften the material underneath. Then scrape it off with a stripping knife.

Alternatively You can cover a textured coating with a thin skim of plaster, or by attaching battens to the wall and putting up sheets of plasterboard, but these are both expensive options. For a quicker and cheaper DIY solution, a smoothing compound is now available, which can be applied to an entire wall or ceiling with a wide flexible knife.

SAFETY NOTE Never sand a textured coating – either with a power tool or by hand. Many old coatings contain asbestos which is dangerous if inhaled.

Stripping washable, heavy relief and painted paper

Wallpaper that has been covered with paint can be removed in the same way as standard wallpaper, but the coating must be scored vigorously to allow the water to penetrate.

Tools Bucket; sponge or old paintbrush; wide stripping knife; water; wallpaper paste; washing-up liquid; scoring tool.

1 Score the surface with a serrated scraper or orbital scorer so that water can soak through into the paper. Do not use a wire brush or wire wool – small pieces of metal may become embedded in the plaster and cause stains on the new paper surface.

2 Apply water and strip the covering as for standard wallpaper.

Vinyls and easy-strip papers

1 With a fingernail or knife blade, lift a corner of the covering away from its backing paper.

2 Peel the covering away from the backing, keeping it as close as possible to the wall. If you stand back and pull the strip of top paper towards you, it may pull the backing paper with it.

3 If the backing paper is stuck securely to the wall and in good condition, use it as lining paper for the next covering. But if it is damaged or not stuck firmly, strip it off as for standard wallpaper.

USING A STEAM STRIPPER

If you want to strip a room in a day, your best bet is to use a steam stripper.

Tools Steam stripper; wallpaper scorer; rubber gloves; safety goggles; wide stripping knife; dustsheets.

Before you start Cover the area with dustsheets and put on some old work clothes and a pair of rubber gloves. Read the instruction leaflet carefully.

1 Fill the tank, switch the stripper on and wait for the light to come on, indicating that the stripper is ready. This

SAFETY TIP

If you are stripping wallpaper around power points, wall lights or light switches, protect them with plastic bags taped on with masking tape, and switch off electricity at the consumer unit (fuse box) before using water or steam around them.

usually takes about ten minutes, when steam begins to come out of the plate. While you are waiting, score the surface of the paper with a scoring tool.

2 Strip a length at a time, working from the bottom up, loosening stubborn areas with a stripping knife. Hold the plate at the bottom of the length. Keep it in position until the paper shows signs of damp – usually after about a minute.

3 Holding the plate in one hand over the next area you are going to strip, use the other to scrape paper from the first area.

4 Top up the tank as necessary, first switching off and leaving the stripper to cool for half a minute.

TIP Take care when using a stripper on plasterboard. The steam will soften the surface, so use a stripping knife as little as possible and do not dig it in.

Preparing and stripping wood and metal

Whether your woodwork or pipework is brand new or old and coated with layers of paint, it will need some preparation before you decorate. Adding another layer of paint to a door, window frame or radiator will seldom hide imperfections in the layer beneath.

Woodwork

New bare wood
• Look for cracks and blemishes that need filling. Use fine surface filler for interior wood.
• Smooth the wood by hand, using fine abrasive paper, working with the grain. Alternatively, use an orbital or multi-purpose power sander, again working with the grain. Be gentle, because with power tools even the finer grades of abrasive paper remove wood very fast.
• Apply knotting fluid (below) to all visible knots to stop resin bleeding from them.

Old bare wood
• If there are signs of wet rot – soft patches easily penetrated by a penknife blade – then these will need dealing with.
• Fill all cracks and gaps with filler as for new wood. When set, smooth with fine abrasive paper.
• As soon as preparatory work is complete, apply a coat of wood primer.

FOLLOW THE CONTOURS

Preserve the definition of wooden mouldings by rubbing them down as little as possible. Remove as much old paint as possible with scrapers and homemade tools – for example, a small metal washer held with mole grips for concave areas (above). Then finish with fine abrasive paper wrapped around a suitable base – for example, a piece of wooden dowel (below). Alternatively, use an abrasive sponge block.

Painted wood

If paint is sound and in good condition, do not strip it unless the thickness causes an obstruction – making windows hard to open, for instance. Instead, clean with sugar soap and water. This removes dirt and keys the existing paint so that new paint will adhere to it.

Keying (roughening a gloss surface very finely) is essential; without it new paint is easily damaged and scratched off.

Where paintwork is slightly damaged but mainly sound, only work on the damaged areas. Rub with a damp flexible sanding pad to remove all loose material, wipe clean and allow to dry. Prime bare wood where it is exposed. Then lightly rub the whole area with very fine abrasive paper and wash with sugar soap, as for sound paintwork. Fill small chips with fine surface filler.

If you need to remove all the paint, you can use chemical strippers or a hot-air gun (see pages 16–17) or a blowlamp.

Varnished wood

Use a chemical paint stripper or varnish remover to get back to bare wood.

Stained wood

If the wood is to be painted and the stain is old, rub down with a flexible sanding pad. If the wood is to be sealed to give a natural finish, remove the stain with a wood bleach. Follow the instructions on the label.

Wood treated with preservative

Coat the wood with an aluminium primer-sealer. Otherwise the preservative may bleed through.

Metalwork

New iron and steel

Wipe off grease with lint-free rag, then use abrasive paper to remove rust and wipe clean. Apply metal primer.

Old rusted iron and steel

• Wear safety goggles and leather gloves for protection.
• Use wire brushes and abrasive paper to remove all rust.
• Fill any serious pitting with epoxy-based filler. If it is left untreated, rust can eat through thin metal, leaving holes. This quite often happens to old steel window frames.
• Epoxy-based filler is a rust inhibitor, so it can be applied to sound surfaces still showing signs of rust discoloration.
• Before painting the metal, apply a metal primer. This contains zinc to prevent further rusting. Different primers are available for different types of metal.

Aluminium alloy and anodised aluminium (such as windows and patio doors)

These materials have a very shiny surface and, in good condition, do not need painting. But if you want to match a decorating scheme, clean them first with white spirit, dry off and then apply enamel paint direct. No primer or undercoat is necessary.

Copper (such as central heating pipes)

Remove any protective grease with white spirit and rub away any discoloration with fine abrasive paper or wire wool. Wipe clean, then apply gloss paint or enamel paint direct. No primer or undercoat is necessary. Ordinary gloss can withstand the heat of water passing through the pipes.

Stainless and chromium-plated steel

This should not require painting but, if desired, apply gloss paint or enamel paint direct after removing any grease with white spirit.

Painted metal window frames

Do not interfere with sound paint on metal, unless a build-up of paint is making frames too tight. If the paint does not need stripping, clean down the frames with sugar soap and water. Key the surface with fine abrasive paper or wire wool, then apply a primer and gloss paint.

Where rust is lifting paint

This may be found in older houses where window frames were not galvanised. Wear safety goggles and brush away flaking paint with a wire brush. Scrape back the remaining paint to reveal bright metal. Do not ignore any hidden rust; it can lead to a new attack. Treat with rust inhibitor, apply a metal primer and paint with gloss.

HELPFUL TIP

If you don't have a proprietary gel-type paint stripper, you can mix a little wallpaper paste into a water-based liquid one.

Stripping poor paintwork

Paint can be stripped with the help of chemicals or heat – often it is best to use a combination of methods. If wood is to be repainted, you won't have to strip off every bit of paint, as you must if you want to varnish the wood.

Using a hot-air gun

A hot-air gun will soften paint so that scrapers can remove it more easily. Some have an attachment to shield glass from heat when stripping window frames. Because of the risk of fire, do not put any newspaper on the floor. Instead, keep a steel tray (an old baking sheet is fine) below to catch paint peelings. Wear cotton gloves (rubber gloves will make your hands too hot from the heat caused by the gun).

1 Soften the paint by moving the hot-air gun backwards and forwards. The heat is very strong so do not concentrate in one area or you may burn the surface. The paint should soften in seconds.

SAFETY TIP

Any pre-1960s paintwork is likely to contain lead. Wear gloves and a face mask when stripping old paint. Seal the waste in a bag and contact your local council for details of how to dispose of it – don't burn it.

2 Strip the paint from flat areas with a broad-bladed scraper. Push the tool away from you or upwards. When scraping a vertical surface, make sure your hand is not immediately below the hot paint, which may drop onto it.

3 When using a shave hook on mouldings, hold it at an angle, so that hot paint cannot fall onto your hand.

4 If you accidentally scorch the surface, rub fine abrasive paper along the grain to remove charred wood.

5 Apply a wood primer and paint.

Paint strippers

Chemical strippers are good at removing paint completely from wood, especially if you want to varnish it. Most are applied in liquid form or as a paste. They are useful for stripping window frames, where heat could crack the glass. However, this method can be slow and costly. Always neutralise strippers – as directed on the container – before redecorating.

Using liquid strippers Wear safety goggles and protect your hands with rubber gloves. If you spill any on your skin, wash off immediately. Open all the windows because these products give off strong fumes.

1 Use an old paintbrush to apply liquid stripper. The paint wrinkles and breaks up about 15 minutes after application. Give the stripper enough time to work – if you try to strip the paint too soon it will not come away and another application of stripper will be needed. If you leave it too long, it will dry and begin to harden again.

2 Remove the paint using a shave hook on moulded surfaces – pulling the tool towards you.

3 On flat surfaces, push a wide scraper away from you. A heavy build-up of paint will need more than one application.

GEL STRIPPERS

Use paste or gel strippers on vertical surfaces. They will not run on to the floor, are easier to control and more effective. Protect the surrounding area with newspaper. Apply the stripper in a thick coat, which will slowly dry on the surface while the chemicals work beneath. Follow the manufacturer's instructions; it is usually best to cover the paste with cling film and occasionally spray it with water. After the recommended time (hours rather than minutes), scrape away the paste – it will bring the old paint with it.

Removing tiles from walls and ceilings

Leaving tiles in place and painting or tiling over them is often the easiest option, but if you want a flat finish for painting or wallpapering the tiles will need to be removed.

Ceramic tiles

Tiles in older houses may be stuck to the wall with cement mortar – sometimes 15mm thick. If you remove them you will probably need to have the wall plastered before you can decorate. Tiles stuck with adhesive are easier to get off, but they may pull plaster with them. In this case, the surface will need to be made good.

Tools Heavy duty gloves; safety goggles; dust mask; wide steel masonry chisel (bolster); club hammer; paint scraper. Possibly also: power sander.

Before you start Put on safety goggles and protective clothing – splinters of glass from the glaze will fly in all directions as you chip away at the tiles. Close doors to prevent dust escaping from the room.

1 Prise the tiles away from the wall one at a time with a bolster chisel and a club hammer. Some will come away in one piece, others may crack and break. There is no easy technique – continue to chisel until you have removed all of the tiles.

2 Use a sharp paint or wallpaper scraper to remove any adhesive left on the wall. If the tiles were stuck with cement mortar you will need to continue chipping with the bolster chisel.

Polystyrene tiles and cork tiles

Tools Wide stripping knife or bolster chisel; safety goggles; possibly a hot-air gun.

1 Lever tiles away from the surface using a wide stripping knife or bolster chisel. They are more likely to break into pieces than come off whole. Although the tiles will come away easily, adhesive – which is difficult to remove – will remain.

2 Use a hot-air gun to apply heat direct to the remaining glue and then scrape it off with a stripping knife.

Choosing fillers

A huge range of fillers is available, with new ones brought out all the time. Here are the main ones.

Hairline crack filler For fine cracks in plaster, plasterboard and painted surfaces.
• Liquid filler applied by brush from a tin.
• Dries white in 10 minutes.
• Not suitable on damp surfaces.
• Fully dry in 24 hours.

Paste filler For cracks up to 2mm, small blemishes indoors and gaps in wood.
• Comes in tubes and tubs.
• Surface dry in 30–60 minutes; rapid repair versions dry in 5–20 minutes.

Internal plaster repair Gives a smooth finish to damaged plaster surfaces.
• Sold in ready mixed and powder form.
• Fill deep holes (over 50mm) in layers.
• Dry in 24 hours.

Exterior filler General filling for external masonry, concrete and paving.
• Available ready mixed or as powder.
• Sets in 1 hour and is drillable.
• Dries to a grey, weatherproof finish.

All-purpose filler For cracks and holes in most materials, inside and out.
• Powder or paste; some types are mixed with a diluted adhesive for outside use.
• Dries to a tough, weather-resistant surface that should be painted.
• Do not expose to permanent damp.

Polyester-based metal filler Cracks in metal gutters and downpipes.
• Chemically bonded filler and catalyst.
• Quick setting – use within 5 minutes.
• Can be sanded after about 20 minutes.

Wood fillers Repairs cracks and small holes in wood, inside and out.
• Solvent-free paste in tubes and tubs.
• Comes in various wood colours.
• Sets in about 10 minutes; can be sanded, drilled and stained.
• Epoxy-based wood fillers are very strong. Use to any depth; they can be drilled, screwed or planed when dry. The chemically bonded filler and catalyst is quick-setting, so use within 5 minutes.

Frame sealant Fills gaps between masonry and window or door frames.
• Flexible, rubbery paste applied from container fitted into cartridge gun.
• Forms a skin after about 4 hours and can then be painted.
• Available in white and other colours.

Foam filler Largely used for holes or gaps round pipes through a wall, inside or out.
• Sticky foam applied to dampened surface from pressure spray.
• Expensive but good for awkward areas.
• Workable for about 5–7 minutes.
• Expands to 60 times its original volume and moulds to fit shape of hole. Can be cut, sanded and painted when dry.

Using wood filler

The type of wood filler you choose depends on whether the wood is going to be painted or simply waxed or varnished.

Wood must have a well-prepared surface before the final finish is applied. This means filling any holes before the wood is finally sanded smooth. If the wood is to be left its natural colour, buy a wood filler that matches. If it is going to be painted, fill with an interior filler.

Tools Filling knife; abrasive paper; electric sander.

Materials Interior filler or wood filler.

1 If you plan to paint the wood, use a power sander with fine abrasive paper to key existing paintwork. Then wash it with a solution of hot water and sugar soap.

2 If you are repainting the area, use interior wood filler to fill any defects such as cracks or dents. Be sure to press the filler in firmly and scrape away any excess.

3 Once the filler has set hard, sand it smooth ready for painting.

4 If you intend to apply a finish through which the wood can be seen – stain, wax or varnish – then sand it smooth and fill it with a wood filler (known as stopping) that matches the colour of the bare wood as closely as possible.

5 Press the stopping into the holes and cracks, taking care not to spread it into the surrounding grain.

6 Wait until the stopping has dried to the same colour all over – usually about 30 minutes – then sand it flat.

Filling small holes and cracks

Small cracks, dents, holes or gouges in plaster walls or ceilings can be repaired with interior filler.

Tools Old paintbrush; filling knife; abrasive paper and block, or power sander. Possibly also: trimming knife; large paintbrush; cold chisel; garden spray gun; length of wood.

Materials Suitable filler.

1 Rake out the crack with a filling knife. If the crack is in plasterboard and the paper surface has been torn, cut off jagged edges with a sharp trimming knife.

2 Brush the crack with a dry brush to remove dust.

3 Load filler onto the end of the filling knife blade and draw the blade across the crack. Scrape the excess off the blade, then draw it down the crack to remove excess filler from the wall and smooth the surface.

4 For deeper holes, build up the surface in layers, working from the edges. Wait about two hours for each layer to dry before applying the next.

5 When the filler is completely dry, smooth it to the level of the surrounding surface with medium or fine abrasive paper wrapped round a wooden block, or use a power sander with fine-grade sandpaper.

Filling awkward gaps and holes

Some holes cannot be filled properly with standard interior fillers. You can buy special fillers to deal with them.

Flexible mastic

Gaps between walls and window frames, skirting boards, door frames and staircases, move. Therefore they should be filled with a flexible mastic that sticks well and resists cracking. The mastic is applied with a cartridge gun.
• If the cracks are deep, half-fill them with thin strips of expanded polystyrene before applying the sealant.

• Make sure the sealant reaches to both sides of the gap. Press it in and smooth the surface with a wetted fingertip.

Foam filler

Deep cavities – around a pipe through a wall, for example – can be difficult to fill but the job is easier if you use foam filler. Wear the gloves supplied – the foam is very sticky until it sets.

Before you start Experiment to see how fast the foam comes out of the nozzle and how much it expands.

1 Brush any dust out of the hole and dampen the surface with water.

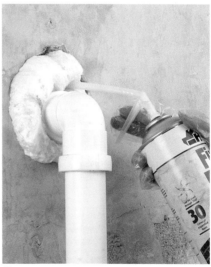

2 Allowing for expansion, release foam into the hole. You may only need a thin bead.

3 Leave the foam for 1 to 2 hours. When it has set, cut any excess away with a hacksaw blade or a sharp knife. Wear a mask to avoid inhaling the dust.

Painting

Tools for painting

As with all tools, quality counts. Buy the best painting tools you can afford and take care of them.

Brushes Good quality brushes improve with use, as the tips become rounded and any loose bristles come out. Cheap brushes usually contain far less bristle for a given width, and they are often badly anchored so that the bristles tend to fall out. Only use cheap brushes for applying wood preservatives to rough timber or removing dust after sanding down.

Radiator brush Bristles are at an angle to the handle for painting awkward places, such as behind radiators and pipes.

Synthetic fibre brushes Bristles are locked in so that they don't drop and are easy to clean. They are especially suitable for water-based paints. Use 12mm, 25mm or 50mm brushes for painting woodwork and 100mm or wider for walls and ceilings.

Angled cutting-in brush This brush is useful for window frames as its angled tip helps you to get close to the glass without getting paint on it.

Paint kettle Pour paint into a paint kettle as required. The kettle has a handle, unlike most small paint tins. Line the kettle with foil before pouring in the paint. This can be removed and thrown away after use.

Paint shield Use a plastic or metal shield to keep paint off glass when painting window frames. You can also use one to prevent your brush from picking up dirt from a floor when painting a skirting board.

100mm brush

50mm brush

25mm brush

12mm brush

Cutting-in brush

Radiator brush

Rollers An easy way to spread emulsion paint over large areas is with a roller. A metal or plastic tray is needed for loading the roller with paint.

Foam rollers These are good general-purpose rollers if a fine finish is not important. They can only be used on smooth and lightly textured surfaces. Patterned foam rollers will apply textured paint in relief over a smooth surface.

Sheepskin rollers Synthetic sheepskin makes a good all-purpose roller for covering large areas with emulsion. Will cover uneven surfaces, such as woodchip.

Mohair rollers The very fine pile of mohair rollers (which are mostly synthetic) gives a high-quality finish. Suitable for paints with a sheen, such as silk emulsion and gloss.

Radiator rollers Small rollers on a longer handle are useful for painting areas difficult to reach, such as behind radiators.

Extension handles Most rollers have a hollow handle that will take a telescopic extension pole so you can reach the tops of walls or ceilings without using a stepladder.

Radiator roller and changeable head

Roller tray and sheepskin roller

Roller frame

Patterned foam roller for textured coating

Sheepskin roller sleeve

Fine foam roller sleeve

Mohair roller sleeve

Telescopic extension handle for roller

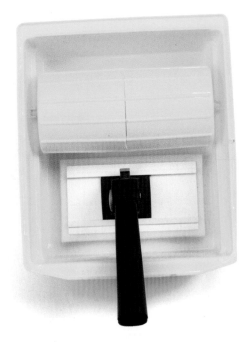

Paint pads A paint pad is the best choice for applying thin coats of paint to smooth surfaces easily and without drips. Pads vary in size from about 25mm square up to a width of 180mm and also come in useful shapes, such as a crevice pad or corner pad, for painting awkward areas or shaped mouldings. Edging pads have wheels that roll along an adjacent wall or ceiling to give a clean straight join where cutting in with a brush would be fiddly. You need a tray for the paint. Like rollers, some pads have hollow handles for extension poles.

150mm
paint pad

Corner pad

Crevice pad

75mm paint pad

What goes on before the paint?

Most surfaces require a preparatory coating to make sure they are stable and sealed before you can apply any paint. Be sure to choose a coating suitable for the surface and consider whether it is indoors or out.

Take special care with any painted surface that will be exposed to the weather. The end grain of wood must be thoroughly soaked with primer to prevent the rain from penetrating. Primer by itself is not particularly weather-resistant, so do not leave a primed surface exposed to rain and wind for long. Cover it with an undercoat and a topcoat as soon as possible.

New windows, doors and other wooden fittings are usually supplied ready primed. Check for scratches and other damage and prime any areas that have become exposed. Give a second coat of primer to any areas that will become hidden by brickwork after the fitting is installed.

All bare or new wood needs a sealing coat of primer before it can be painted. First, coat any knots with knotting (see opposite). Then apply a wood primer or an all-purpose acrylic primer. This is water-based and dries fast. When using a microporous paint on bare wood, no primer or undercoat is needed. Do not apply more than two coats.

Stick to separate coats
Primers are designed to seal surfaces, while undercoats obliterate underlying colour and provide a strong key for the protective top coat. Using a combined primer/undercoat may save time and money, but you will generally not get results as good as those achieved with separate coats.

Primer choice
A primer specially formulated for a particular surface – plaster, wood or metal – will last longer and produce a better finish than a universal primer. Copper pipe needs no primer, but an undercoat may be necessary to hide the colour of the metal.

Choosing primers and other sealers

Knotting
• Paint onto resinous areas, especially knots, in wood.
• Prevents resin in wood from seeping out and discolouring paint.
• When dry, coat knotting with primer.

Primer
• Apply to new or bare wood, plaster or metal.
• Seals pores in absorbent surfaces and forms a key to which other coats grip.
• Buy primer for a specific surface or use all-purpose primer.
• Prime bare plaster with proprietary sealer or a coat of emulsion diluted to one part water and four parts paint.

Primer-sealer
• For stained walls and plaster, old bituminous coatings and areas treated with preservative.
• Contains fine scales of aluminium and forms a barrier to seal the surface.
• Proprietary stain-blocks are available in aerosol form and are ideal for small areas.
• Apply a second coat if stain is still visible after the first has dried.

Stabilising solution
• Sometimes used to seal distemper.
• Binds together surfaces to provide a firm support for paint.
• Apply fungicide before stabilising solution on a mould-affected surface.

Fungicide
• Kills mould on any affected surface.
• When spores are dead, brush them away and apply another coat.

How much paint do you need?

Work out how much paint you need before you buy any at all. It's better to overestimate than underestimate, to be sure that you can complete a job with paint from just one batch.

Most paint tins indicate the average area their contents will cover, but the table below offers a rough general guide. Porosity, texture and the base colour of the surface will affect the amount you need. Highly porous surfaces, such as bare plaster, will absorb a lot – especially when priming. Rough surfaces, such as woodchip or pebbledash, are also very thirsty. Two or three undercoats may be necessary to cover a very strong colour, and always allow for at least two topcoats for good protection against the weather on external surfaces.

Pick healthier paints
Water-based paints and varnishes have a lower volatile organic compound (VOC) content than solvent-based ones. This means they do less environmental damage and pose less of a health risk to people using them regularly. Use products with a low VOC rating if solvent-based paints give you nausea or headaches. Information about VOCs is now often given on the tin.

COVERAGE PER LITRE

Coating	Coverage
Primer	8–12m²
Undercoat	16m²
Gloss	14m²
Non-drip gloss	12m²
Emulsion	10–13m²
Masonry paint	5–10m²

To calculate the area of a large surface, break it down into smaller parts, numbered 1–6 on this plan. Multiply the height by the width of each part and add all the totals together to get the final area.

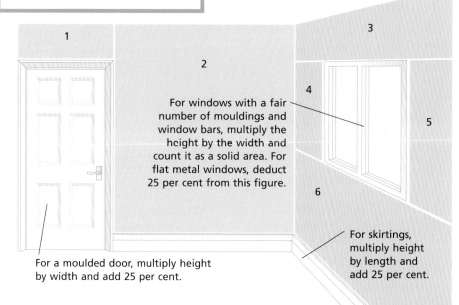

For windows with a fair number of mouldings and window bars, multiply the height by the width and count it as a solid area. For flat metal windows, deduct 25 per cent from this figure.

For a moulded door, multiply height by width and add 25 per cent.

For skirtings, multiply height by length and add 25 per cent.

Choosing paint

Before you buy paint, study colour charts, or buy some tester pots to try out on the wall. Paint tends to look darker once it is applied, so if you are doubtful about which shade to buy, choose the paler one.

Solvent-based paint, or gloss, is used for wood or metalwork and water-based emulsions for walls and ceilings. Solvent-based paint must be used with an undercoat, but this is not necessary for emulsion. Water-based gloss paints are also now available. They are faster to dry and easier to clean, but tend to give a less glossy finish.

Modern 'thixotropic' paints are jelly-like in consistency and ideal for less experienced decorators, as they will not drip. They may be more expensive per litre, but seldom need an undercoat or second topcoat, so may not cost more in the long run.

Solid non-drip emulsion is sold in wide shallow trays designed to take a standard decorating roller – they are ideal for painting ceilings.

The final coat of paint – the topcoat – can have a gloss, semi-gloss or matt finish. Other names for semi-gloss include eggshell, silk, satin and sheen. The glossier the paint, the tougher and more durable the surface will be. Also, look out for moisture-resistant paints developed for kitchens and bathrooms.

Common types of paint

Undercoat
• A full-bodied paint with more pigment than topcoat and good covering power.
• Used on primed surfaces, before applying topcoat, or on dark surfaces that will be painted a paler colour.
• Apply a second coat if undercolour shows through the first coat.
• Wash brushes with white spirit.

Solvent-based gloss
• Used for woodwork and metalwork. Gloss is suitable indoors and out, though some are specially designed for exterior use.
• Can also be applied to walls and ceilings.
• On wood, always use with an undercoat.
• Apply two thin coats, rather than one thick one.
• Clean brushes with white spirit.

Water-based gloss
• Used for woodwork and furniture.
• Dries much faster than solvent-based gloss.
• Gives a hardwearing finish; glossy, but not as shiny as the solvent-based equivalent.
• Clean brushes with water and detergent.

Non-drip or one-coat paint
• Used for interior woodwork.
• Combines undercoat and topcoat and stays on the brush well.
• Two coats may be needed when covering a dark colour.
• Clean brushes with white spirit.

Emulsion
• Water-based paint used for walls and ceilings.
• Dries quickly and does not leave brush marks.
• Can be diluted with 20 per cent water to form its own primer for bare plaster.
• Use a roller for fast coverage.
• Two or three coats may be needed.
• Clean tools with water and soap or detergent.

Anti-condensation paint
• The best paint to use in bathrooms and kitchens as it will not peel away when exposed to a lot of steam.
• A semi-porous emulsion that absorbs moisture in the air and allows it to evaporate as the air dries.
• Often contains fungicide to deter mould.
• Apply in the same way as emulsion.
• Clean tools with water and detergent.

Textured (plastic) coating
• Can be applied to walls and ceilings with uneven or unattractive surfaces.
• Much thicker than paint: it forms a permanent coating which is extremely difficult to remove.
• Apply with a shaggy roller, unless the manufacturer specifies otherwise.
• Coat with emulsion once dry.
• Clean tools with white spirit.

Masonry paint
• Used for render and pebbledash.
• Two main types: textured and smooth.

Other special paints
There are also special paints for floors, tiles and melamine (for revitalising kitchen units). Matt black is used for beams and blackboards; radiator enamel stays white when hot; anti-damp paint seals in minor surface dampness.

Painting techniques

A paintbrush is a versatile tool. Use one for applying gloss to wood and metalwork and for painting where colours or surfaces meet – around windows and doors, for instance.

Using a brush

1 Stir the paint – unless it is non-drip. Make sure any liquid on the surface is thoroughly mixed into the paint by lifting the stick as you stir.

2 Choose a brush which is the right size. As a rough guide, paint window frames with a 25mm brush, door panels with a 75mm brush, and walls and other large surfaces with a 100mm brush. Grip large brushes around the handle and hold smaller brushes more like a pencil.

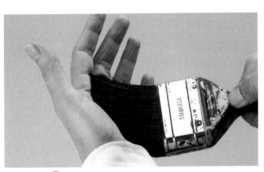

3 Flick the bristles against your hand to remove dust and any loose bristles.

4 Dip the brush into the paint to about one-third of the bristle depth. Press the brush against the tin or kettle wall to remove surplus paint. Do not scrape the brush over the rim of the kettle because too much paint will come off.

USING OLD PAINT

Wipe the rim before you open an old tin of paint. If a skin has formed, cut around the edge and lift it out. Stir the paint well and then strain it through an old stocking to remove any bits of hardened paint.

HELPFUL TIP

Line a paint kettle with aluminium foil – to make cleaning easier – and pour in paint to fill about one-third of the kettle. Do not work from the tin; you may contaminate the paint with dried paint, dirt and possibly rust from around the rim.

Painting with non-drip paint

Do not stir non-drip paint and do not remove any excess paint from the brush; it is meant to be heavily loaded. Apply the paint in horizontal bands. Don't overbrush or the paint will run.

Painting a textured surface

When painting a surface with a heavy texture or relief, load the brush with more paint than for a smooth ceiling or wall. This cuts down the time it takes to coat the surface and fill all the little indentations. But dip to only a third of the bristle depth.

If you are painting a relief wallpaper, Anaglypta for example, use a brush as wide as you can comfortably manage without putting too much strain on your wrist. A 100mm paintbrush is ideal. With a textured coating on a wall or a ceiling, you can use a shaggy pile roller (see page 32).

Painting with gloss

1 Start at the top of the surface. Paint three vertical strips parallel with each other, leaving a gap just narrower than the brush width between the strips.

2 Do not reload the brush. Working from the top, brush across the painted area horizontally to fill the gaps and smooth the paint.

3 With the brush now almost dry, lightly go over the section you have just painted with vertical strokes to ensure an even coating, stopping on an upward stroke. This is called 'laying off'.

4 Using the same technique, paint a similar sized section underneath the one you have completed. Work the wet paint into the dry.

Painting with emulsion

1 Start at the top of the wall. Apply the paint in all directions, working horizontally across the surface and moving down when one band is complete. Do not put the paint on too thickly.

2 Lay off the paint with light brush strokes and a fairly dry brush, working in a criss-cross pattern. Finish off with light vertical strokes.

'Beading' where colours meet

Where walls meet the ceiling and where adjacent walls are of different colours, keep the meeting edge as straight and as neat as possible. Do not rush the job.

1 Turn the paintbrush edge on, holding it like a pen.

2 Load the brush with enough paint to cover about one-third of the bristle depth.

3 Press the brush flat against the surface so that a small amount of paint (the bead) is squeezed from the bristles. Work towards the edge gradually, rather than trying to get close immediately.

4 Draw the brush sideways or downwards along the surface, keeping your hand steady.

Cutting in

Achieve a neat finish along wall and ceiling edges by first painting the edges with a brush, before switching to a roller or pad.

1 Paint four or five overlapping strokes at right angles to the edge.

2 Cross-brush over the painted area in a long, sweeping motion, keeping parallel with the edge.

Using a roller

You can cover an area more quickly with a roller than with a brush, but you may need to apply more coats because the paint goes on quite thinly. Use a foam or mohair pile on a smooth surface and a lamb's-wool or nylon pile on a textured one.

1 Thoroughly stir the paint (unless it is a non-drip or solid roller paint).

2 Fill about one-third of the roller tray with paint. Do not overfill, or it will spill.

3 Dip the roller into the paint, then run it lightly on the ridged part of the tray. This spreads the paint evenly on the roller sleeve.

4 Push the roller backwards and forwards, alternating diagonal strokes at random.

5 Do not apply too much in one coat. And do not work too fast, or paint will be thrown off the sleeve and spatter. Try not to press the roller too hard or paint will be forced off the ends in ridges.

6 Use a small paintbrush to cut in the edges around doors, windows, corners and where walls meet the ceiling.

Using a paint pad

Paint pads are suitable for applying water-based paints. They quickly cover large areas like walls and ceilings and will cope with lightly textured surfaces.

1 Stir the paint and pour some into a flat tray or the speed tray sometimes supplied.

2 Run the pad backwards and forwards on the roller in the speed tray or hold the pad flat against the paint in the tray. Do not let it sink below the pile level. If the pad absorbs too much paint it will drip. A pad needs to be reloaded more often than a brush or roller.

3 Start painting, moving in all directions with a gentle scrubbing action. Work in strips four times the width of the pad.

4 Do not press too hard or paint may be forced off the pad in drips. With practice you should get no drips at all.

CUTTING IN WITH A PAD

As an alternative to using a brush to obtain a neat finish along wall and ceiling edges, try using an edging pad with guide wheels, which is designed for the job. The wheels guide the pad along the ceiling line as you push it along the wall.

Dealing with paint problems

The main causes of paint breaking down are incompatible paints being applied on top of one another, poor preparation of the surface, damp or trapped moisture, grease, rot or rust.

Runs Too much paint applied in a thick coat results in runs that are hard to disguise.
• If the paint is still wet, brush out runs; but not if the paint has started to dry. Instead, wait until it is completely dry and then rub down with very fine abrasive paper until the surface is smooth.
• Clean with a damp rag.
• Apply a new thin topcoat.

Insects on painted surface Don't try to remove small insects that become trapped on gloss paint when it is still tacky. Wait until the paint is dry, then rub them off with a rag dampened with white spirit.

Paint on glass The best tool for removing paint from a window pane is a plastic scraper fitted with a trimming knife blade. The blade should be inset very slightly so it cannot mark the frame.

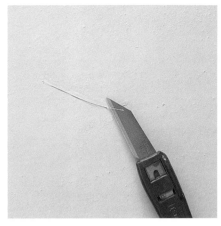

Dropped bristles Unless you spot a stray bristle as soon as it appears and can lift it off the paint before it gets stuck, wait until the surface is thoroughly dry before trying to remove it. Then carefully cut it away from the new paintwork with a scalpel or sharp craft knife.

Gritty paint surface If a newly painted surface feels rough and gritty, paint has been applied with a dirty brush or has become contaminated by the surrounding areas. Or there may have been bits of skin in the paint. Strain old paint through a paint strainer or a pair of tights. Use a paint shield or piece of card to guard against picking up dirt from a floor.
• When a gritty surface is dry, rub smooth with damp wet-and-dry abrasive paper, wipe clean, then apply a new coat of paint.

Crazing (sometimes called orange peel) When a paint surface breaks up like mini crazy paving, incompatible paints have been used. The top layer of paint breaks up because it expands at a different rate from the one underneath.
• Usually, you must strip the paint with chemicals or a hot-air gun and start again.
• Rub down very small areas – no more than a few centimetres square – with a flexible sanding pad or with wet-and-dry paper damped with water.
• When the surface is smooth, fill the stripped area with a fine surface filler, prime and repaint.

Blistering Prick a blister – if water emerges, damp is trapped under the paint or is finding its way in from behind.
• Strip the blistered paint with a hot-air gun and leave the wood until it has dried.
• Prime the surface and then repaint the whole of the repaired area.

Flaking

The paint has not been keyed to the surface, which may be too smooth (as with old gloss paint) or may be chalky (as with untreated distemper). Alternatively, rotting timber may be pushing the paint off or rust may have formed underneath.
• Strip small areas by rubbing with fine abrasive paper, fill with a fine surface filler, apply a primer and repaint.
• Larger areas must be completely stripped and prepared again from scratch.

Stains

Stains occur when water in emulsion activates impurities in a wall; areas rubbed with a wire brush or wire wool develop rust stains; or deposits in an unlined flue come through the paint surface.
• Prevent stains by applying an aluminium primer-sealer before you start painting.
• If the problem occurs afterwards, brush a primer-sealer over the stain and then repaint.

Mould and discoloration

Spores settling on paintwork that is damp – possibly due to condensation – often lead to mould patches.
• Treat the affected area with a fungicide as directed by the manufacturer, wash the surface clean, let it dry and then repaint.

Loss of gloss sheen

Gloss paint will sink into the surface and lose its shine if the surface was not primed – or if either primer or undercoat was not left to dry completely.
• Rub down with damp wet-and-dry abrasive paper.
• Brush off the dust and wipe with a clean, damp rag, then apply a new topcoat.

Paint will not dry

The room is badly ventilated or very cold.
• Open all the windows and doors or put a heater in the room.
• If this does not solve the problem, the paint has been applied to a dirty – and probably greasy – surface.
• Strip it off with chemical stripper or heat and start again, taking great care to clean the surface thoroughly.

Wrinkled paint

Usually caused by applying a second coat of paint before the first has dried. Solvents in the wet paint underneath attack the second coat when they try to pass through it and make it wrinkle.
• Strip the paint with a chemical stripper or heat and redecorate, this time allowing each coat to dry before applying the next.

Visible under-colour

Liquid gloss does not have good covering power, so always use undercoat to hide a strong colour.
• Put on another layer of topcoat, but switch to a one-coat paint, which has more body and covering power.

Dark patches on painted wood

Knots in wood which have not been sealed before you decorate may ooze resin when the sun warms them, and the resin will force its way through the paint film.
• Strip paint away with the edge of a scraper blade, then with fine abrasive paper to expose the knot.
• Brush knotting over the area to seal it, leave it to dry and repaint.

COPING WITH SPILLS

Act fast if you spill paint. Scrape up as much as you can with a flat-bladed tool. Then dab off what's left with dry absorbent cloths and paper before lifting the last traces with clean cloths dampened with cold water (for spilt emulsion) or white spirit (for solvent-based paint). Use washing-up liquid on a damp cloth to remove traces of white spirit from fabric.

Attack dried emulsion paint on carpets by repeatedly dampening the stain and teasing lumps of paint out of the pile with an old toothbrush. A water-based paint stripper may successfully remove dried solvent-based paint from carpets and hard floor surfaces. Test it on an inconspicuous corner first. Neutralise the stripper residue with water immediately afterwards.

Looking after brushes, rollers and pads

Always thoroughly clean paintbrushes, rollers and pads after each painting session. Use cold water to wash off water-based paint immediately and never leave any of your painting tools to soak in water.

Before you start Check on the paint tin to see what solvent is needed. Some paints require special thinners to remove them. Buy the necessary solvent at the same time as you buy the paint. Emulsion and acrylic-based paint need only plenty of clean water, plus soap or detergent. Other paints may need white spirit. You can also use a proprietary brush cleaner.

Leaving a brush loaded with paint

Pads, rollers and trays must not be left loaded with paint, but you can keep a wet brush or roller sleeve for an hour or two so long as you wrap it in aluminium foil or a plastic bag to keep out the air and prevent the paint from drying.

Cleaning a brush

1 Gently scrape excess paint from a brush onto paper. Use the back of a knife and work from the heel (the base of the bristles) to the tip.

2 Wash emulsion paint out of a brush under a running tap. Rub a little soap or washing-up liquid into the bristles and rinse in clean water.

3 Clean off a solvent-based paint with white spirit or proprietary brush cleaner.

4 All brushes will benefit from a final wash in soap and a rinse in clean water. Use your fingers to work out any remaining paint. Once a brush is clean, shake it vigorously outdoors to get rid of excess water.

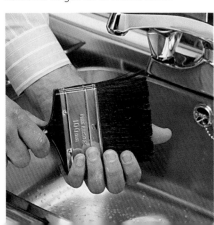

5 When the paintbrush is dry, slip a loose rubber band over the tip of the bristles to hold them together and keep the brush in shape.

Cleaning a roller

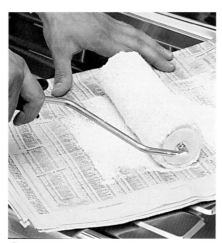

1 Run the roller over the ribbed part of the paint tray and then over sheets of newspaper to remove excess paint.

2 Remove the roller sleeve if possible. Wash under running water, working the paint out of the sleeve with your hands.

Cleaning a paint pad

1 Run the pad over paper to get rid of most of the paint.

2 Wash the pad in clean water, taking great care not to separate the mohair from the base. The process will be faster if you use a little soap, but make sure you rinse it all out in clean water.

Storing brushes, rollers and pads

Leave clean brushes and rollers to dry and then wrap them in brown paper or lint-free cloth, such as old sheeting. Store the tools flat in a warm dry place.

Paint pads are an awkward shape to wrap, so store them in sealed plastic bags to keep off dust.

Reviving a neglected brush

A brush that has not been cleaned well after use will become hard. The best way to soften a brush is to use a proprietary restorer, following the instructions on the pack. Tease out any paint particles in the base of the brush with a fine brass suede brush. Only use a restored paintbrush for rough work, like applying primer.

Storing paint

It is worth holding on to leftover paint as it may be needed for touching up. Follow these storage tips and you'll be able to keep the paint for months.

Keep paint fresh

Use a piece of kitchen foil to prevent a skin forming on the top of an opened tin of paint. Using the lid as a guide, cut a circle of foil just large enough to cover the surface of the paint. Press it down gently to exclude air trapped beneath it.

Tipping a tin of paint upside down for a few seconds before storing it also helps to stop a skin from forming. The paint flows around the underside of the lid to form an airtight seal when the tin is turned the right way up.

Store leftovers in jars

A small amount of paint will keep better if you decant it from the tin into a jar with a screw-top lid. Make sure you have enough paint to fill the jar, or a jar small enough to just take the paint, so there's little room for air. Rub some petroleum jelly around the neck of the jar before pouring in the paint; then any paint that spills over won't make the lid stick fast. Remember to label the jar for future reference.

Disposing of paint

When you finish using a water-based paint, wipe as much of it as possible off brushes and rollers before rinsing them in the sink, so that as little as possible is washed down the drain. Unwanted water-based paint can

A QUICK WAY TO FILTER OUT THE GRIT

If there's grit in the paint, stop it getting onto your brush by tying a piece of material cut from a pair of old tights over the rim of the tin. Use the tip of the brush to push the material down into the paint, so that clean paint rises up through it. The same trick allows you to filter contaminated paint back into a clean container before storing it.

be sealed in its tin and put out for the refuse collectors. Never pour used white spirit or solvent-based paint down the sink or into a drain. Contact your local authority to enquire about their safe disposal facilities.

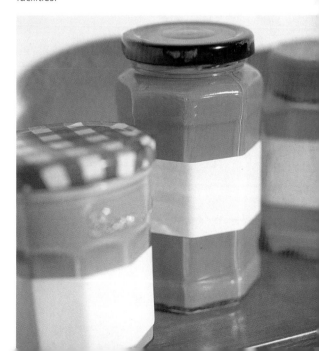

Painting everything in the right order

When painting a room, plan your work so that you cover the area efficiently and avoid spoiling newly painted surfaces with drips and spatters.

Ceiling before walls

Emulsion the ceiling first, so that any splashes on the walls are covered later. Start to paint a wall at the top right-hand corner if you are right-handed, from the opposite corner if left-handed.

Frames before paper

Paint door and window frames before hanging wallpaper, so there's no chance of getting paint on the paper.

Brush the margins

If you are going to paint the ceiling or adjoining walls in different colours, use a brush for the edges first, then a roller to infill the rest of the surface.

Bands and strips

Apply paint in horizontal or vertical bands, then blend the parallel bands together. Paint walls and ceilings in strips about 500mm wide, working quickly so that the edge of the paint doesn't get a chance to dry. Finish off around door and window frames after the rest of the wall is covered. Turning the heating off and closing windows will extend the drying time – worth doing if you have a large room to paint.

Every other tread

Paint or varnish every other tread when decorating an uncarpeted staircase, and identify which can be walked on by taping sheets of newspaper over them. Adapt the same method when painting or varnishing a floor you need to use all the time, doing half one day and the rest the next.

HELPFUL TIP

It is a good idea to paint the ceiling (which can be a messy job) even before stripping any wall coverings. This is the only exception to the rule that all preparatory work must be done before you start painting.

IF THE WALLS ARE TO BE PAPERED

When a room is to be papered, take about 15mm of paint onto the wall around door and window frames, above skirting boards and below any picture rail. Then, if you leave any small gaps in the papering, the paint will show through, making the imperfection less obvious.

WHEN TO PAINT COVING

If you paint coving and ceiling roses after you have painted the ceiling, you will avoid getting splashes on the new paintwork. If coving is to be the same colour as the ceiling, paint it before you paint the walls, otherwise it is easier to paint coving at the end of the job.

Keep it neat

Avoid making splashes with a roller by pushing it slowly; don't snatch it away at the end of each pass. Try not to overload the brush when painting a ceiling. Dip just the bottom quarter of the bristles into the paint; then it won't seep into the ferrule and run down the handle – a common problem when painting ceilings.

Safety first

Protect eyes

Wear safety spectacles when painting a ceiling. They will protect your eyes from paint splashes when you look upwards.

Protect hands

Wear a pair of fabric gloves while painting, especially when using solvent-based paints. They save having to remove paint from your hands with white spirit, which can irritate the skin. A barrier cream will help to stop paint sticking to your skin if you prefer to work without gloves.

Be height conscious

Use a stepladder that is high enough for you to reach the ceiling without stretching or standing on the top rung. In a stairwell, a combination ladder is useful. A stepladder can also act as a trestle for a scaffold board. Borrow another stepladder or hire a trestle for the other end of the board, which must be at least 38mm thick.

You can hire scaffold towers to use in some stairwells. The tower must be vertical, so take time to adjust the feet. Never reach forwards from a scaffold tower, or lean sideways from a ladder or stepladder.

Painting walls and ceilings

If surfaces have been sufficiently prepared, the job of painting is fairly straightforward. Make sure that carpets and any furniture that has to remain in the room have been covered with dustsheets or newspaper to avoid any damage from stray paint. Also ensure that the room is well ventilated before you begin.

Painting a ceiling

Make sure that you can safely and comfortably reach the area you are decorating. Use a scaffold board supported by trestles or stepladders. Your head should be about 75mm from the ceiling.

If you do not like working at a height, you can use an extension handle (or broomstick) fitted to the hollow handle of a roller or pad, for most of the painting. But you will need to stand on steps or a board to cut-in where the walls and ceiling meet and around the tops of doors and windows.

Paint the ceiling in strips starting near the window. If there is more than one window in the room, begin nearest the one where most light comes in. Cut in the edges as you work.

Painting a wall

When using a roller, paint horizontal bands about 500mm wide across the wall. Work from the top to the bottom. With a brush, paint blocks about 500mm square. Start in the top right corner (or the top left one if you are left-handed). Paint the blocks from the top of the wall down and then across.

Painting different surfaces

Bare plaster Dilute emulsion to one part water and four parts paint and use it as a priming and sealing coat. Follow this with at least two coats of full strength emulsion. Use a foam or mohair roller or a paintbrush or pad as large as you can comfortably work with. Do any touching up with a small paintbrush while paint is still wet.

Paper Lining paper is the ideal surface for painting, as it hides small cracks and blemishes. Apply at least two coats of paint, using whichever tool you prefer. Do not worry if small bubbles appear on the paper. They disappear as the paint dries.
• Paint high relief papers such as Anaglypta with a shaggy pile roller.
• Old wallpaper can be painted but does not give great results. Test an area first to see that the paper does not bubble or come away from the wall. If it does, you must strip the wall, but if not, apply full-strength emulsion as the first coat. The less water getting onto the wall the better. Use a roller, pad or brush.
• Do not paint over wallpapers that contain a metallic pattern – the pattern tends to show through the paint.

Painted surface New emulsion paint can be applied straight onto old provided the surface has been washed down. If there is a drastic colour change, two or three coats will be needed. Never paint over distemper – it must be removed (page 10). As a general rule, do not paint walls or ceilings with gloss; it enhances blemishes in the surface and is prone to condensation If you want to paint an old gloss surface, first rub it down with a flexible sanding pad or fine wet-and-dry abrasive paper, damped with clean water. This destroys the glaze on the paint and helps the new paint film to grip the old. Wipe away dust before painting.

Power through it A power roller makes light work of covering large areas of wall with emulsion. Paint is fed continuously along the hollow extension pole by a pump, so you never need to stop to reload the roller. Keep the roller moving to avoid drips and runs. Power rollers can be hired.

Textured coatings Use a brush or shaggy pile roller to put on the paint; you will find that emulsion gives the best result. Textured coatings are sometimes abrasive so they may rip foam rollers and can be difficult to coat thoroughly.

Ceiling tiles Paint polystyrene tiles with emulsion, as long as they are clean. Use a roller, and a small brush for the joins between the tiles. Never use a gloss paint – it creates a fire hazard when it is put on expanded polystyrene. If you plan to stick polystyrene tiles on the ceiling, it is much easier to paint them before you put them up, especially if they have chamfered edges.

Painting walls with glazes

A glaze is a thin, almost transparent film of oil-based colour. The oil slows the glaze's drying time but you still have to work fast. Glazes can be put over surfaces coated with a matt or eggshell solvent-based paint, but will not adhere to a gloss finish.

You can sponge, rag, drag or stipple a glaze, using normal household materials – such as old cloths – or specialist products. Good stippling and dragging brushes are expensive, but cheaper versions may give poor results. Whichever technique you choose, the surface must be thoroughly prepared, as glazing will highlight any imperfections.

You can buy transparent oil-based glaze, called scumble glaze, which varies in shade from pale to mid-brown. As a rough guide, a 2.5 litre tin of glaze will be enough to cover all the walls in a room 3.5m x 3.5m.

Tinting the glaze

Use artist's oil colours or universal stainers to tint the glaze to the colour you want. This is a matter of trial and error, which becomes easier with practice.

1 Blend a small blob of colour – a little goes a long way – with white spirit. Add this to the rest of the glaze in the paint kettle, stirring all the time to mix them well.

2 Test the result on the surface to be painted and add more of the same or a different colour until you are satisfied.

3 Glaze is usually diluted with some white spirit before you apply it. The consistency should be about the same as single cream.

4 If the glaze thickens as you work (because the white spirit has evaporated) stir in some more white spirit. Be careful: too much will weaken the colour.

Alternatively You can achieve similar painting effects with eggshell solvent-based paint instead of a glaze.
• Mix one part paint to two parts white spirit. It is best to choose white paint and then to tint it to the required colour.
• Blend a blob of colour with white spirit, add it to the paint mixture and try out the results until you achieve the right colour.
• This 'glaze' dries quickly so it is more suited to sponging and ragging than to dragging or stippling.

You can also produce decorative effects with emulsion paint – one part diluted with three or four parts water – but this dries even faster. Tint the emulsion paint with water-soluble paints (gouache, acrylic or poster paints) and dilute the emulsion with water, not with white spirit. Always apply an emulsion 'glaze' over an emulsion base coat – not a solvent-based one.

Protecting the surface It is advisable to protect a decorative paint finish with varnish. Make sure the glazed surface is completely dry (this may take 24 hours or longer) before you do so. Buy varnish with as little colour in it as possible and choose a finish depending on how glossy you want it to be. You may need to apply two coats.

Sponging a wall

Glaze applied to the wall with a sponge produces a soft, dappled effect.

Tools Real (not synthetic) sponge; paint kettle, flat paint tray or baking tin; rags, rubber gloves.

Materials Glaze tinted the desired colour; white spirit.

1 Thin the glaze with white spirit in the paint kettle, stir well and pour some into the flat tray. Wear rubber gloves to protect your hands. Dip the sponge into the glaze and squeeze out the excess.

2 Dab the sponge onto the wall – do not press too hard. Work in a circular pattern to prevent the prints from becoming too regular and vary the position of the sponge on the wall so that the impressions it makes are not all the same.

3 Reload the sponge as the glaze runs out and wash the sponge in white spirit when it becomes saturated with glaze. Squeeze it out well or you will over-dilute the glaze.

4 For a marbled effect, leave the surface to dry and then sponge on a second colour, using the same technique as before.

SAFETY TIP

Glaze is highly flammable. Never leave rags soaked with glaze lying around – they may suddenly burst into flame without warning. When you have finished with a rag, do not keep it to use again – always use a clean rag. Put used rags in a tin with a tightly fitting lid and throw it away. Never put used rags straight into a dustbin.

Ragging a wall

With ragging, the pattern is irregular, rather than even, which makes it one of the easiest and fastest decorative techniques.

Tools A large supply of lint-free rags (all the same texture); 100mm paintbrush; paint kettle; rubber gloves.

Materials Glaze tinted the desired colour; white spirit.

1 Pour the glaze into the paint kettle and thin it with white spirit.

2 Brush glaze onto the surface, beginning at the top of the wall and covering a strip about 500mm wide down to the floor.

3 Bunch up a rag into a ball and dab it over the surface to pick up glaze while it is still wet. Use one or both hands to move the rag in all directions. This is a messy job so wear rubber gloves. You may find it easier if you crumple one rag into a ball and then wrap another rag around it.

4 Change the rag whenever it becomes full and too wet to pick up more glaze. It is also a good idea to unwrap the rag and crumple it again in a different way so that the patterns you make are not all the same.

5 Continue to apply and rag off glaze until the whole wall is covered.

HELPFUL TIP

Always mix up more glaze than you think you need – it is impossible to match a colour if you run out halfway through the job.

Dragging a wall

This technique will show up the slightest imperfection in a surface, so it is best kept for only the smoothest walls. If possible, try to get someone else to brush the glaze onto the wall, while you drag it off immediately afterwards.

Tools Paint kettle; 100mm paintbrush; brush with extra-long bristles (called a flogger) or another wide, coarse-haired paintbrush; clean lint-free rags.

Materials Glaze tinted the desired colour; white spirit.

1 Thin the glaze with white spirit in the paint kettle. It should be a thin, cream-like consistency – if it is too thick or if one of the bristles in the brush is bent, some of the dragged lines of glaze may break into droplets and spoil the effect.

2 Start in a top corner and apply a strip of glaze about 500mm wide, from the top of the wall to the bottom.

3 Again, moving from the top down, drag the dry flogger through the glaze. You may need to stand on steps to reach the top and climb down carefully as you drag the wall.

4 Keep the movement flowing and as straight as possible. However, the results will be more successful if you relax and do not concentrate too much on keeping the lines steady.

5 Do not worry if the lines are slightly crooked in places – they will not spoil the effect from a distance. Hold the flogger against the wall with light, consistent pressure.

6 If you cannot drag the whole wall in one movement, break off and then brush from the bottom up to where you stopped, overlapping slightly at the join. If you have to do this with the next strip as well, break off at a different height, so that you do not get a line running across the wall where the joins meet.

7 Wipe the flogger frequently on a lint-free rag so that the bristles remain as dry as possible and do not lose their shape.

Stippling a wall

This technique creates a uniform, soft effect. The special brush required can be bought from specialist paint shops and larger builders' merchants. Use a white or pale base coat for best results. As with dragging, speed is essential so it is easier if you have a helper.

Tools Paint kettle; stippling brush; 100mm paintbrush; clean lint-free rags.

Materials Glaze tinted the desired colour; white spirit.

1 Pour the glaze into the paint kettle and thin it with white spirit.

2 Brush the glaze onto the wall in a vertical strip about 500mm wide.

3 Go over the wet area with the stippling brush, stabbing at the surface. Keep the bristles at right angles to the wall, otherwise the brush will skid.

4 Wipe the brush clean on a dry lint-free rag as the picked-up glaze accumulates on the bristles, otherwise they will begin to stick.

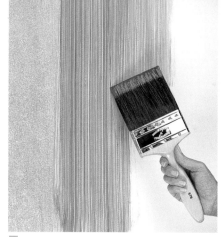

5 Continue the process in strips across the wall.

6 Clean the brush immediately after use with white spirit, followed by a little washing-up liquid and warm water.

Stencilling

Using stencils is a quick and easy way of decorating furniture, walls and floors. Buy stencils pre-cut, or make your own.

Tools Stencil brushes.

Materials Plastic stencils; paint; low-tack (easily detachable) tape or spray adhesive; masking tape; paper towel.

1 Position the first stencil and secure it with tape or low-tack spray adhesive.

2 Use masking tape to cover any cut-outs within the stencil that you intend to paint with another colour.

3 Hold the stubby head of the brush at right angles to the stencil and dab paint onto the cut-out areas, working outwards from the centre of each cut-out.

4 Wait until paint is dry to the touch, then repeat the process for the next colour.

Painting woodwork

Once the ceiling and walls are painted, move on to the woodwork, which should have been well prepared before you started work on the walls and ceiling. Whatever the surface, the order of painting remains the same.

Tools Paintbrushes; abrasive paper; wood sanding block; thin piece of wood; dusting brush; lint-free cloth or tack rag.

Materials Filler for wood painted indoors; knotting; primer; undercoat; topcoat.

1 Brush a coat of knotting solution (see page 14) over any resinous areas or knots in the wood so they are sealed and resin cannot seep through.

2 Apply an even coat of primer to bare wood and leave it to dry.

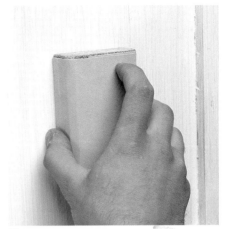

3 Use fine grade abrasive paper wrapped around a block of wood to rub lightly over primed areas to remove any rough bits.

4 Remember to sand moulded areas as well. Use abrasive paper round a thin piece of wood, or a flexible sander.

FOR A PERFECT FINISH

Always sand wood smooth and fill any holes before painting.

1 Wrap a piece of abrasive paper around a wood sanding block and rub it along the grain of the wood.

2 Use a fine brush to remove all the dust, brushing in the direction of the grain to clear all crevices.

3 Press filler into the holes, taking care not to spread it into the surrounding grain. When the filler has dried to the same colour all over sand it flat and dust once more.

1 Apply the paint in thin coats, so that it does not form drips or runs. Let the paint dry between coats.

5 Put one undercoat on light surfaces and two on dark ones. Use an undercoat appropriate to the colour of the paint.

6 When the undercoat is dry, gently rub with abrasive paper. Remove dust with a dusting brush. To pick up remaining dust, wipe with a damp lint-free cloth (a clean old handkerchief is ideal) or a tack rag impregnated with resins that remove dust.

7 Apply the topcoat with a brush that is an appropriate size for the surface.

Painting cornices and mouldings

Plaster or imitation plasterwork cornices and ceiling roses can be painted with emulsion to match or contrast with the ceiling and walls. Or pick out details in a second colour. Never use gloss paint on polystyrene coving – it creates a fire hazard.

2 If you are using two colours, either paint the raised parts first or paint the whole area and fill in the recesses, when dry, with an artist's sable brush.

3 To keep your hand steady, lean on a mahl stick (a signwriter's rest). To make a mahl stick, pad the end of a piece of dowel with sponge or cotton wool wrapped in a lint-free rag.

Tools 25mm brush with no straggly bristles; artist's sable brush; mahl stick (see right).

Materials Emulsion paint(s).

Before you start Make sure the surface is clean and smooth. Fill small cracks in plaster with interior filler, wait for it to dry and then rub down with fine abrasive paper. If a part of the cornice is broken away, repair it before you do the painting.

VARNISHING WOODWORK

Avoid bubbles Don't scrape the loaded brush against the rim of the tin or across a string tied across a paint kettle. Instead, just load your brush and then press it against the side of the container. The excess varnish will drip off the brush.

Reduce shine If wood looks too shiny after varnishing, you can reduce the sheen with fine wire wool. Rub gently, with the grain, to cut back the gloss so that there is hardly any reflection at all. This is particularly suitable for pale woods.

Add colour Using a tinted varnish rather than a clear one will add colour without permanently staining the wood. There are wood shades and paintbox colours available. Before you start, test the tint of the varnish by painting patches of one, two and three coats of varnish on a piece of spare wood. If the tinted varnish is slightly too dark, add a little water to acrylic varnish or white spirit to polyurethane, and then paint more patches to see if the colour has lightened sufficiently.

Colour match fillers If you need to fill wood that is to be varnished, buy a wood filler that will match the colour of the finish. Fillers are made in a limited colour range, so look at the filler colour chart in the shop and choose the nearest. If you can, take a piece of the wood with you but do not match the wood against wet filler; the filler will become paler as it dries.

Using waxes and oil finishes

Wax and oil finishes are most often used on furniture and wood with a natural finish, where the grain of the wood is visible. Oil finishes are best suited to wood that will be subjected to moisture and frequent handling. Wax is easier to apply but the surface must be completely smooth and clean before application. Most finishes are safe to apply but always read the manufacturer's instructions first.

Applying an oil finish

Tools Plastic cups; foam brushes; clean lint-free rags; abrasive paper; latex gloves.
Materials Oil finish.

Before you start Spread out plenty of newspaper in the work area. Most oil finishes are non-toxic but wear latex gloves and dispose of used rags and brushes in an airtight container as they can spontaneously combust if left crumpled in a ball.

1 Strip off any old finish and sand the wood until smooth. Start with 80 grit paper, then 120, and finally finish with 180 grit paper, sanding in the direction of the grain to remove any scratch marks.

2 Dust off then wipe down the surface with a tack rag or a cloth, which has been sprinkled with a little linseed oil. Turn the cloth often to expose a clean surface.

3 Use a foam brush to apply a coat of oil in the direction of the grain. Avoid over brushing and do not stop halfway through the job or a line will appear in the finish.

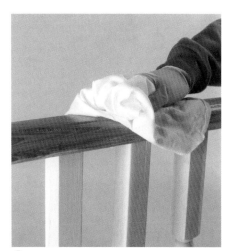

4 After 15 minutes use a clean rag to wipe any excess oil from the surface. When one rag becomes saturated replace it with a clean one.

5 Leave the oil to soak in for 3 hours then apply a second coat and wipe down as before.

6 Leave for 24 hours and then use a soft clean cloth to buff to a smooth shine.

HELPFUL TIP

Waxes and oils will alter the colour of the wood, so test them on a scrap piece of wood or on an area that will not be visible before you start the job.

Applying a wax finish

Tools Abrasive paper; soft cloths; latex gloves.

Materials Wax; acetone or denatured alcohol.

1 Strip off any previous finishes and sand the surface smooth. Make sure that you remove any surface imperfections and scratches that will show through the finish.

2 Wipe down the surface with acetone or denatured alcohol to remove any residual surface-impurities.

3 Immediately rub on the wax, as detailed in the manufacturer's instructions. Be careful not to apply too much; two thin coats are better than one thick one.

4 Use a soft lint-free cloth and buff to a smooth shine until all the wax has penetrated into the surface of the wood.

Painting doors and door frames

Doors have several faces and grain patterns going in different directions, each of which needs to be painted separately in a particular sequence for a good finish. Always open a door before you paint it. Leave the door frame until last.

Tools Suitable brushes; perhaps cutting-in brush; paint shield.

Materials Masking tape; wire wool; white spirit; knotting; primer; undercoat; topcoat.

Before you start Take off any door furniture, put down a dust sheet and hold the door open with a wedge on either side. It's a good idea to keep the door handle nearby in case the door closes.

USING TWO COLOURS

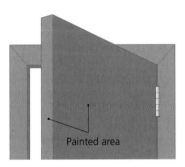

Painted area

1 If the door is painted a different colour on each side, paint the lock edge the same colour as the side of the door which opens into the room.

Painted area

2 Paint the hinge edge of the door so that it is the same colour as the adjacent, visible face of the door.

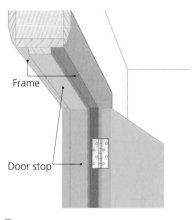

Frame

Door stop

3 If the door frame is also painted a different colour on each side, all the parts which can be seen from one side when the door is open should be painted the same colour.

In general, you don't have to paint the top and bottom edges of a door. However, if the top edge is overlooked (from a staircase, for example) paint it, so it does not stand out as bare wood.

Panelled doors

Paint the sections of the door in the sequence illustrated, for best results.

Use a brush of a suitable size to paint each part of the door – use a smaller one for the mouldings than for the panels, for instance.

Do not overload the mouldings with paint; this is a common cause of drips and runs. Keep the brush lightly loaded.

Glass-panelled doors

Use a paint shield, an angled cutting-in brush or masking tape to keep paint off the glass. Whichever you use, allow paint to go onto about 2mm of the glass to seal where the glass and frames meet.

Paint the rest of the door with a broader brush – about 75mm wide. To avoid drips, do not overload the brush with paint.

If gloss paint gets on the glass, remove it with a rag damped with white spirit before it dries. If paint dries on the glass, scrape it off with a glass scraping tool.

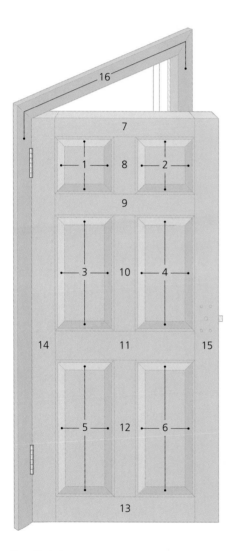

Panelled doors Paint the panels and the mouldings, then the rest of the surfaces.

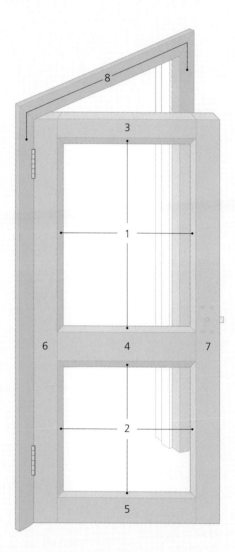

Glass doors Paint the moulding around the glass before the remainder of the door.

Painting wooden mouldings

Skirting boards and picture rails are usually painted with gloss to match any other painted woodwork in the room. Balustrades are painted to match doors and other woodwork in the hall. If the walls are to be papered, paint woodwork first.

Tools Suitable brushes; pieces of old card.
Materials Paint; white spirit.

Before you start Fill damaged woodwork with fine surface filler then rub down to give a smooth finish ready for painting – gloss paint is unforgiving of imperfections and will show up every chip and dent.

Skirting boards

If you can, lift fitted carpets before painting a skirting board. When the carpet cannot be lifted, protect it with dust sheets.

1 The gap between the skirting board and the floor is likely to be full of dust. To remove the worst of it, vacuum along the skirting board before beginning. Then use a piece of card to stop the paintbrush from touching the floor.

2 Apply paint with a 50mm or 75mm paintbrush, depending on the height of the skirting board. Brush lengthways along the run of the board.

Picture rails

1 With a 25mm brush, paint two or three thin coats, not one thick one, allowing each coat ample time to dry.

2 Finish off with fine brush strokes along the run of the picture rail.

Balustrades

The wooden uprights and handrail of a staircase balustrade suffer a lot of wear and tear. It may seem like a fiddly job, but giving them a fresh coat of paint will help to keep them in good condition.

Tools Bucket; cloths; paintbrushes; filling knife.

Materials Sugar soap; fine abrasive paper; white spirit; fine surface filler; wood primer.

Before you start Make sure that all the uprights (balusters) are secure and in sound condition, and prime any areas of bare wood.

1 Wash down the woodwork with a sugar soap solution before you paint. Grease and dirt will have collected, particularly on the handrail, and will prevent the new paint from taking hold. Use fine abrasive paper to key the surface all over, then wipe it with a little white spirit.

2 Start by painting the balusters, working from the top of the staircase down, and from the top of each one in turn. Don't overload your brush with paint, or you will end up with drips and runs. If the balusters are turned in an ornate shape, let your brush follow the curves to apply paint to all the recesses.

3 You will need to move round the balustrade to paint from the staircase side as well to make sure that each baluster is completely covered.

4 Once you have painted all the balusters, move on to the handrail. Paint the underside first then give the top and sides of the handrail two coats of paint to give it a hard-wearing finish. Allow the first coat to dry thoroughly and rub it down lightly with fine abrasive paper before applying the second coat.

5 Paint the newel posts after the handrail, working from the top down and making sure that any recesses on a decorative finial at the top are well covered.

6 Finish by painting the strings – the edges of the staircase. Paint the outer string first, and any panelling that reaches down to the ground floor, then lift the carpet on the stairs and paint the inner side.

Paint balustrades in this order: **1** balusters; **2** handrail; **3** newel posts; **4** outer string and wall panelling; **5** inner string

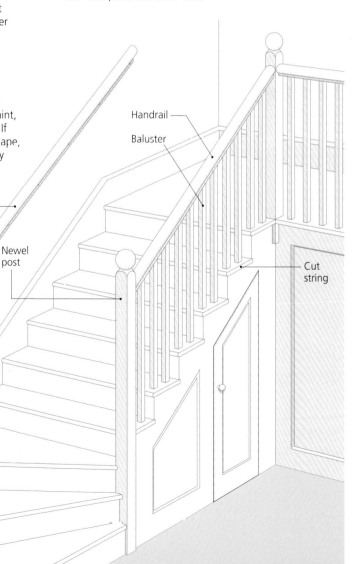

Handrail

Baluster

Wall-mounted handrail

Newel post

Cut string

String

Painting windows

It nearly always takes more time to paint a window than you think, because of the number of surfaces and because you have to keep paint off the glass. For security reasons, you will probably want to close windows at night, so start work as early in the day as possible.

Tools 25mm or 50mm brush or an angled cutting in brush; paint shield.

Materials Masking tape; wire wool; white spirit; primer; undercoat; topcoat; cling film or talcum powder.

Before you start Put down dust sheets, and protect the glass with masking tape. Fix the tape about 2mm from the frame so that a thin line of paint goes onto the glass. This will seal any gap between the glass and the frame. Or use a masking shield, moving it along as you paint and cleaning it regularly.

Casement windows

1 Open the window. Paint the frame in the order illustrated (right). Do not apply too much paint in one coat or it will run and take longer to dry.

2 The painting sequence is largely determined by the fact that the brush strokes should follow the construction of the joinery; so the vertical brush strokes will 'cut off' the horizontal ones.

3 Keep paint off handles and stays. These look best cleaned up and left natural. Remove any dried paint splashes on metal with wire wool dipped in white spirit.

4 If you have to close casements and the paint is touch-dry but not absolutely hard, rub a little talc on the meeting surfaces. Alternatively, place a sheet of cling film between the surfaces most likely to stick.

Sash windows

1 Paint the frame following the order shown below. Almost close the window to paint the inside runners; give them a very thin coat to prevent surfaces from sticking.

2 Do not paint the sash cords or they will harden and fail earlier than they should.

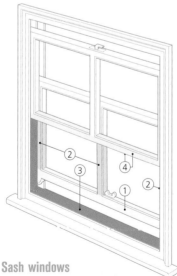

Sash windows
Open sash windows and reverse their positions, then paint in the following order:
1 meeting rail; **2** vertical bars as far as possible; **3** the area that the inner sash sits on, and lower runners; **4** cross-rail and underside.

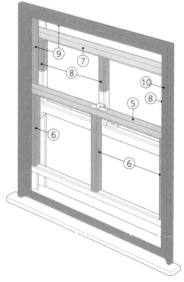

Reverse the windows, then paint:
5 cross-rail; **6** vertical bars; **7** cross-rail; **8** rest of vertical bars; **9** soffit, top runners and behind cords; **10** frame. The colours on the windows indicate the extent of the numbered areas.

Casement windows

Paint casement windows in this order:
1 cross-bars and rebates; **2** top and bottom cross-rails; **3** hanging stile and hinge edge; **4** meeting stile; **5** frame. The colours on the drawing indicate the extent of the numbered areas.

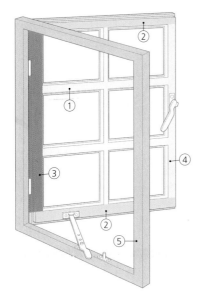

Painting metalwork

Make sure that all metalwork is clean and free from grease before painting.

Windows

Metal windows tend to be tighter fitting than wooden ones, so do not let paint layers build up on them. If the paint layers are very thick, remove the paint with a chemical stripper (page 15). In all other respects, the painting procedure remains the same as for wooden frames (see left).

Radiators

Never paint a hot radiator – always let it cool first. Wait for about an hour after you finish painting, then turn on the heating to speed up the drying process. Special radiator paint is available that will keep its whiteness despite the heat.

Before you start Check for patches of rust or bare metal that may be showing through. Rub them down with a fine wet-and-dry abrasive paper, and then touch them up with metal primer.

1 Apply gloss direct to new and already painted radiators unless there is to be a colour change, in which case apply an undercoat first.

2 Use a 50mm brush and keep the coat as thin as possible to avoid runs. You can paint a flat panel radiator with a small roller; this will not give quite as good a finish, but takes less time.

3 Do not paint over control valves; they must be left free to turn.

Painting metal pipes

1 Make sure that steel and copper pipes are clean and free from corrosion. Use fine wire wool to clean them.

2 Apply gloss paint direct with a 25mm or 50mm brush. There is no need for a primer unless the pipe is lead. Start by brushing up and down, then smooth the paint along the length of the pipe.

3 Never paint over stop taps or controls or they will not work.

Cast-iron fire surrounds and wrought ironwork

1 Rub down and remove any rust (page 17) and prime the metal if necessary.

2 Use a suitably sized brush to coat the surface with gloss or enamel paint direct, without an undercoat.

3 If possible, remove intricate wrought ironwork and take it outside. Then spray it with an aerosol, shielding the area behind. Always use thin coats to prevent runs. Hold the can at right angles to the work and at a distance of about 300mm.

4 Keep the can parallel with the surface – moving up and down or from side to side. Never swing the can in an arc or hold it in one position for any length of time.

5 If you cannot move intricate wrought ironwork, put on two thin coats of gloss with a small paintbrush

Decorating the outside of a house

Paint deteriorates at different rates, depending on how much it is exposed to wind, rain and sun. Check the whole house from time to time for the first signs of deterioration – when gloss paint loses its shine, or when masonry paint becomes powdery to the touch.

Before you start Surfaces should be clean, stable, and stripped if the paintwork is not sound (page 10). Repair damaged areas of a rendered wall and fix gutters if they are not firmly attached to the fascia board.

When to paint The best time to decorate is after a dry spell because paint will not take to a damp surface. Never paint in frosty conditions or rain, and do not paint on a very windy day – or dust and dirt will be blown onto the new paint.

Before you buy the paint If you are going to change your colour scheme, make sure that the new colours will fit in with the neighbourhood, especially if the house is semidetached or in a terrace.

Calculate how much paint you need in the same way as for interior decorating (page 28). Rendered surfaces require more paint than smooth ones. If all the walls are to be painted, estimate the total outside area of the house by multiplying the length of the walls by the height.

The easiest way to measure the height is to climb a ladder against the wall of the house, drop a ball of string from the eaves to the ground, and then measure the length of the string. Work out the combined area of the doors and windows and deduct this figure from the total.

If you are going to paint the pipes and the outside of gutters, multiply their circumference in centimetres by their length. Divide this figure by 10,000 to give an area in square metres.

Which paint to use In general, use exterior grade gloss paint on wood and metal and use exterior grade emulsion or masonry paint on walls.

Alternatively, on bare wood you can use microporous paint, which needs no primer or undercoat. This paint allows trapped air or moisture to evaporate, reducing the risk of flaking associated with hardwoods.

Never put gloss paint over surfaces (mainly pipes and guttering) that are coated with bituminous paint. This tends to be less shiny than gloss and often looks thicker and softer than other paint. If you are doubtful about whether old paint contains bitumen, rub a rag soaked with petrol over the surface. If the rag picks up a brownish stain, the paint is bituminous. Either continue to use bituminous paint or, providing the surface is sound, coat it with aluminium primer-sealer, then paint with undercoat and gloss.

Paint the house in this order

Complete all the preparatory work before you do any painting – but never leave a surface exposed. Protect it with at least a primer and, if possible, an undercoat before you stop work at the end of a session.

Always decorate from the top of the house downwards so that the newly painted surfaces cannot be spoilt. Paint doors and windows last.

1 Bargeboards, fascias and soffits
All these surfaces are painted in the same way, but not necessarily at the same time. Gutters are usually painted the same colour as fascias so it is easiest to paint them immediately afterwards – before soffits, which usually match the walls or windows.
• Apply knotting, if necessary, and primer to bare wood. Put on an undercoat and leave to dry. Use two undercoats if there is to be a colour change.

Safe access is most important: your ladder or scaffold tower must be secure and in good condition. Use the components of a slot-together platform tower to make a low-level, mobile work platform.

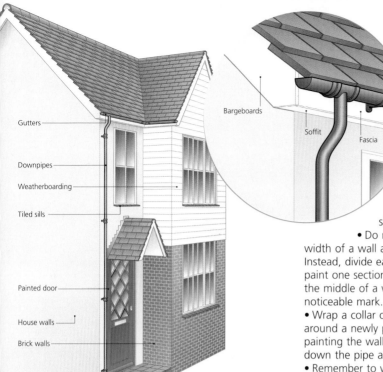

Gutters

Downpipes

Weatherboarding

Tiled sills

Painted door

House walls

Brick walls

Bargeboards

Soffit

Fascia

• On painted rendering – such as pebbledash or a textured surface – no undercoat is necessary. Apply two coats of exterior grade emulsion or masonry paint with a 100mm or 150mm paintbrush or you can use an exterior grade shaggy pile roller.

• Do not try to paint the whole width of a wall along a house in one go. Instead, divide each wall into sections and paint one section at a time. Never stop in the middle of a wall. It will leave a noticeable mark.

• Wrap a collar of paper as protection around a newly painted pipe if you are painting the wall behind it. Move the paper down the pipe as you paint.

• Remember to work safely at high levels, ideally with a helper to steady ladders and pass tools.

4 Brick walls
• Avoid painting good facing brickwork – it is difficult to achieve a satisfactory finish, it cannot be successfully cleaned off later and rarely looks attractive.

• If you really want to paint it, use exterior grade emulsion and a rough surface paintbrush. Apply at least two coats.

5 Windows
Repair a concrete or tiled sill if necessary before painting the window frame.

• Strip paint off wooden sills and make them good, filling holes and uneven areas with exterior grade wood stopping or epoxy-based filler.

• Prepare wood and metal frames as for an equivalent inside frame (page 16).

• Apply knotting to knots and resinous patches in bare wood. Then apply primer, undercoat and exterior grade gloss with a 25mm, 50mm or angled cutting-in brush.

• Paint each type of frame following the sequence on pages 54–55.

• Take special care to seal the joint between putty and glass with new paint. This will prevent rain seeping through the window.

6 Painted doors
• Remove metal handles, knockers and other furniture before painting.

• Prepare the surface as for interior doors (page 14). Use exterior grade gloss to finish; again follow the same sequence and method as described for painting a door inside (page 51).

• Lightly sand with fine abrasive paper to remove any rough bits.

• Apply a coat of gloss with a 75mm paintbrush, finishing with the grain. Leave it to dry for at least 12 hours.

• Apply a second coat of gloss.

2 Gutters and downpipes
• Clean out debris and wash with water and detergent.

• Remove rust from the insides of metal gutters with a wire brush. Wipe the surface with a dry cloth and apply rust inhibitor or metal primer. Paint the inside of gutters with any left-over gloss paint.

• Paint gutters and pipes with exterior gloss using a 50mm brush. If there is to be a colour change, apply one or more under-coats first.

• Hold a piece of cardboard behind pipes as you paint them, to protect the wall.

• Apply a second coat of paint when the first is completely dry.

Plastic gutters and pipes do not have to be painted, but if you want them to match a colour scheme, apply two coats of exterior grade gloss. Do not use a primer or undercoat. If you are leaving plastic gutters unpainted, unclip and remove them while you are painting the fascia boards.

3 House walls
• Areat new rendering that has not been painted before with a stabilising solution or a primer recommended for such a surface.

Wallpapering

Wallpapering tools

For any wallpapering job, you will need a steel measuring tape, a pencil – not a pen – to make marks and a metal straight-edge to act as a guide when you trim paper. Depending on the type of wallcovering, you will need only some of the tools listed below. Have a supply of old towels and sponges to hand for removing paste from skirting boards and for other general cleaning.

Plumb line and bob Use a plumb line to mark the true vertical on a wall before hanging the first length of wallpaper – few walls are straight. Buy one or make one by tying a small weight – a metal nut or a small screwdriver– to a length of string.

Pasting table A folding table – about 2m long and 500mm wide – is the best type because it is easily moved around. As well as being light to carry, the table must be solid enough to stand firmly on the floor.

Water trough If you are using a pre-pasted wallcovering, you will need a trough for wetting each length before hanging.

Paste brush Use a 125mm or 150mm brush to apply paste. If you use an old paintbrush, make sure that it is clean. Wash the brush well in warm water after use.

Plastic bucket Any clean household bucket is fine for mixing the paste. Tie a piece of string across the rim, between the handle anchor points, and rest the brush on the string when you are not using it. Wiping the brush across the string will remove surplus paste.

Paperhanger's scissors

Small scissors

Scissors Paperhanger's scissors with 250mm long blades are best for the main cutting work. The longer the blades, the easier it is to cut a straight line. If possible, use stainless steel scissors because they will not rust. Wipe scissors clean after each use when cutting pasted paper, or the paste will harden on the blades and they will tear the next length. Have a pair of small scissors handy for fine trimming.

Paperhanging brush For smoothing out bubbles and creases in newly hung wall coverings. A large brush – between 180mm and 250mm wide – gives best results. Never use the brush for anything else and take care not to get paste on the bristles.

Paperhanging brush

Seam roller For pressing down the seams of wallcoverings, once they have been smoothed into place. Never use a roller on embossed and relief wall coverings: it will flatten the pattern.

Sponge Use a clean damp sponge to wipe excess paste from the surface of vinyls and washable wallcoverings.

Seam roller

Sponge

Cutting guide

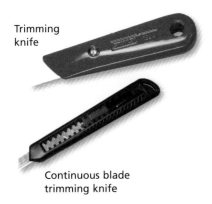

Trimming knife

Continuous blade trimming knife

Cutting guide An L-shaped piece of metal about 500mm long. Hold it against the skirting board, picture rail or coving when trimming lengths of paper on the wall with a very sharp knife. It is an alternative to creasing the paper and trimming with scissors. The correct length of the paper is achieved by tucking the paper into the crease of the guide, which is slightly shaped so that a little extra paper is left on each length. This reduces the chance of leaving gaps between the paper and the skirting board, picture rail or coving.

Trimming knife A knife with a razor-sharp blade is useful for trimming and cutting vinyl wallcoverings. It is also sometimes easier to trim pasted paper neatly with a knife and straight-edge than with a pair of scissors – provided the paper is not too thin. Keeping the knife sharp is essential so make sure that you have plenty of spare blades; or use a knife with a continuous blade that snaps off at intervals to give a sharp new cutting edge.

Choosing paper and paste

Lining paper Plain lining paper is designed to cover poor wall surfaces before they are papered. Sold in five thicknesses, heavier and thicker paper is less likely to tear.
Paste Use cold-water or all-purpose.

Woodchip Useful for covering uneven walls, this paper has two layers bonded together with a sprinkling of wood chippings between them. Paint with emulsion. Rough to the touch, so not suitable in children's rooms or in narrow passages.
Paste Use all-purpose, cold-water, heavy-duty or ready mixed.

Standard wallpaper Quality varies with price: cheap paper is thin and tears easily, especially when damp. It is also more difficult to hang. None of these papers is washable, so avoid using them in kitchens.
Paste Use all-purpose, cold-water or ready-mixed.

Duplex paper The top surface – often with a relief pattern – is bonded to a backing paper. It is strong, easy to hang and holds its shape. Easier to hang than other relief wallpapers.
Paste Use all-purpose, cold-water, heavy-duty or ready-mixed.

Paste-the-wall papers Available in a wide range of colours and designs. They are easy to hang (and strip off) and can be wiped clean. Paste the wall, not the paper.
Paste Use all-purpose, cold-water or ready-mixed.

Relief wallcoverings Heavy papers, such as Anaglypta, embossed with a pattern during manufacture. Suitable for uneven walls and ceilings. Can be painted.
Paste Use all-purpose, cold-water or ready-mixed.

High relief wallcoverings Made from material that feels like hard putty. Many designs available. Lincrusta is more durable than other relief wallcoverings.
Paste Use cold-water, heavy-duty, ready-mixed or Lincrusta adhesive.

Vinyl PVC layer, with pattern or texture, bonded to paper. Durable and washable.
Paste Use all-purpose or ready-mixed (both with fungicide) or vinyl adhesive.

Hessian Available as just a roll of material, or bonded to a backing paper that keeps it from sagging. With unbacked hessian, paste the wall, not the material.
Paste Use all-purpose, cold-water, heavy-duty or ready-mixed.

Silk wallcovering Silk, bonded to a fine backing paper. Expensive and delicate; joins are always visible. Best in small areas.
Paste Use all-purpose, cold-water or ready-mixed.

Japanese grasscloth Made of real grasses, bonded and stitched to a fine paper. Joins are always visible.
Paste Use all-purpose, cold-water, heavy-duty or ready-mixed.

Cork wallcoverings A fine veneer of cork, stuck to a plain or painted backing paper. Colour shows through the holes. Apply paste to the wall, not the paper.
Paste Use all-purpose, cold-water, heavy-duty or ready-mixed.

Metallic wallcoverings Foil bonded to a paper backing. Use only on perfect walls, as any unevenness will spoil the effect. Paste the wall, not the covering.
Paste Use all-purpose or ready-mixed (both with fungicide) or heavy-duty.

Flock wallcoverings Fabric pile, bonded to backing paper. Hang as standard wallpaper but try to keep splashes of paste off the surface. Expensive, but effective.
Paste Use all-purpose, cold-water, heavy-duty or ready-mixed.

Special effects wallcoverings Papers and vinyls in a wide range that give the effect of wood, stone or tiling. Used to create optical illusions. Can be overpowering, and more expensive than standard coverings.
Paste Use all-purpose, cold-water, heavy-duty or ready-mixed.

Choosing the right paste

What you need to know
• Use a paste recommended by the manufacturer of the wallcovering you have chosen. In general, the heavier the wallcovering, the stronger the paste will need to be.
• Many pastes can be mixed to different strengths to suit standard wallpaper or heavy vinyls by adding more or less water. Follow the instructions on the packet.

• Many wallcoverings must be left to one side after they have been pasted to allow the paste to soak into the paper. The paper expands slightly when it is damp and if it is not left to soak it will continue to expand on the wall, making matching difficult and perhaps forming bubbles. In general, heavy, thick coverings need to soak for longer than thin ones. Vinyls need no soaking time because vinyl does not expand when damp.

Glue size Apply to bare wall surfaces before papering. Size adds to the adhesive quality of the paste and makes surfaces slippery so the covering can be slid into place. Mix with cold water. A pack that makes 5 litres will cover enough wall for 8 rolls.

All-purpose paste For all wallcoverings. Powder or flakes are mixed with varying quantities of cold water to suit the particular wallcovering. Follow the instructions on the packet. Contains a fungicide. Water content varies between 4–7 litres per sachet, covering 2–10 rolls.

Cold-water paste The traditional starch-based wallpaper paste, still favoured by many professionals. For all weights of wallpaper, depending on water content. Mix with cold water, stirring well to avoid lumps. Use with glue size, to provide extra slip and adhesion. A 4.5 litre pack will do for 5–6 rolls of medium-weight paper.

Heavy-duty paste For high relief wallcoverings; duplex paper; woodchip; corks; flocks; special effects wallcoverings such as imitation wood panelling; imitation tiling; and imitation brick. Will hold heavy materials. Mix with cold water. A 4.5 litre pack is enough for 4–6 rolls.

Ready-mixed paste For paper and fabric-backed vinyls; paper-backed hessian; grasscloth; special wallcoverings; expanded polystyrene tiles; veneers; coving. Contains a fungicide. Usually supplied in a tub. More expensive than powdered paste. A 2.5kg pack is enough for 3–4 rolls.

Vinyl adhesive For vinyl wallcoverings. A powder or ready-mixed paste containing fungicide to discourage mould – essential when hanging impervious materials. 4.5 litres is enough for 4 rolls.

Lincrusta adhesive For Lincrusta relief decoration and very heavy relief wallcoverings. Thick ready-mixed paste. 1 litre is enough for one roll; 2 litres for 2–3 rolls.

How many rolls do you need?

How much paper you need to buy will be affected by whether the wallpaper design has a pattern that repeats down the length of the roll and must be matched up between lengths. The larger the pattern repeat, the more paper you need and the more wastage there will be.

Most British wall coverings are sold in rolls 10.05m x 530mm, though the size may vary slightly. If your chosen paper has these dimensions, use the chart (right) to calculate how many rolls you need to buy. It is better to have too much paper than to run out and find you can't get any more. You can use any leftover paper for future repair work, or as drawer liners.

Use a steel tape to measure the height of the walls from the skirting board to the picture rail, coving or ceiling.

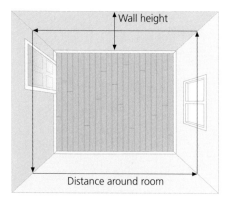

Wall height

Distance around room

When measuring the perimeter of the room, include the width of the doors and all standard size windows – the extra paper will be needed for the trimming at the top and bottom of each length. Only deduct the width of a window from your calculations if it is a French window, occupying a large part of a wall.

If you are papering a ceiling, measure the perimeter of the room and use the chart (opposite).

If you are papering a passage ceiling, measure the width of the ceiling at various places, to make sure it does not vary. Divide this measurement by the width of a roll.

A narrow passage, less than a metre wide, will need only 2 widths. A wider passage may need 3 widths.

Measure the length of the passage, multiply it by the number of widths, and you will be able to work out how many rolls you will need.

Tips on buying wallpaper

Remember the repeat
If your chosen paper has a random pattern – a sponging effect for example – or if it is plain stripes, you will need fewer rolls of paper than if there is a pattern with a drop between the repeats. Pattern repeats vary from around 75mm to 500mm or more. The pattern repeat length is generally noted on the wallpaper wrapper.

If the paper you have chosen has a large repeat, you will probably get one fewer full length out of each roll than you think, so always buy an extra roll or two. Some stores will allow you to return unused rolls if they are left unopened and you have retained your receipt.

The majority of patterned wallpapers have a straight pattern match: the same part of the design occurs along both edges, which means that each length you hang starts at the same point of the design as the length beside it.

Wallpapers with a drop pattern match have the design offset by half the pattern repeat on the two long edges of the paper. Therefore matching lengths of paper as you paste them on the wall uses up more paper. A way to reduce the amount of wallpaper wasted in this way is to cut alternate lengths from two rolls.

HELPFUL TIP

For your first attempt at paperhanging, choose a wallpaper with no pattern match (or with a random pattern) so you have one less thing to worry about as you hang each length.

Special coverings
If you choose from a Continental or American pattern book – or have decided upon a special wall covering, such as hessian – check the size and use the chart provided in the pattern book to work out how many rolls you need. Rolls may be wider than standard wallpaper.

HOW MANY ROLLS DO YOU NEED?

Estimate the number of rolls you will need, including the areas covered by doors and windows. Always buy a little extra to allow for experimentation and mistakes. This chart gives results based on standard 10.05m x 530mm rolls.

Walls

Wall height in metres	Measurement round room in metres										
	10	11	12	13	14	15	16	17	18	19	20
2.0 to 2.2	5	5	5	6	6	7	7	7	8	8	9
2.2 to 2.4	5	6	6	6	7	7	8	8	9	9	9
2.4 to 2.6	5	6	6	7	7	8	8	9	9	10	10
2.6 to 2.8	5	6	7	7	8	8	9	9	10	11	11
2.8 to 3.0	5	5	7	8	8	9	9	10	11	11	12

Ceilings

	Measurement round room in metres						
	9-12	13-15	17-18	20-21	22-24	26-27	29-30
Rolls needed	2	3	4	5	7	9	10

Keep to one batch

Check that all the paper comes from the same batch, to avoid colour variation between rolls. If you have to buy rolls with a different batch number, because the store does not have enough from the same batch, aim to use them in areas where any slight shading variations will not show, such as behind furniture, tucked away in a corner or in a passageway.

Lining paper

Lining paper can improve the end result of your wallpapering immensely. It comes in five thicknesses, and is often twice the length of a roll of ordinary wallpaper. So check the length on the roll and work out how many rolls you will need – you will buy too much if you assume that you need the same number of rolls as the wallpaper you choose.

HELPFUL TIP

Choose a textured or embossed wallpaper if you need to disguise minor imperfections in a wall that is sound but slightly uneven. Smooth wallpaper tends to highlight every surface defect.

Hanging standard wallpaper

Papering the walls is normally the last stage in decorating. Once you have mastered the simple techniques, the job is quick and easy.

Tools Pasting table; bucket; brush; paper-hanger's brush; steel tape measure; plumb line; pencil; wallpaper scissors and small scissors; sponge; seam roller.

Materials Size; wallpaper paste; wallpaper.

Before you start Size bare walls to prevent them from absorbing paste from the wallcovering. Size also makes the surface slippery so that the covering can be slid into place. You can either buy size or make up a dilute solution of the paste you plan to use to hang the wall covering.

Apply size with the paste brush or a short-pile paint roller to cover the whole surface and spread the size evenly. If the size gets onto painted woodwork, wipe it off immediately with a damp cloth.

Cutting paper to length

1 Take a roll of paper and check which way the pattern goes. Decide where definite motifs should be in relation to the top of the wall.

2 With a steel tape, measure the wall height down to the top of the skirting board. Add an extra 100mm for trimming at the top and bottom.

3 Unroll the paper on the pasting table, pattern-side down, measure the length and draw a line with a pencil and straight-edge across the back.

4 Cut along the line with a pair of long-bladed scissors.

5 Turn the paper over, unroll the next length and match the pattern by placing it edge to edge with the first length. Using the cut length as a measuring guide, cut off the second length.

Continue in this way until several lengths are ready for pasting. Number them on the back so that you know the hanging order, and note which end is the top.

Pasting the paper

1 Lay the cut lengths on the pasting table, pattern side down.

2 Position the top piece of paper so that all the spare paper hangs off the table to the right. If you are left-handed, reverse all the following paper-hanging procedures.

3 Adjust the paper so that the long edge aligns with the edge of the table.

4 Load the paste brush and wipe off excess paste by dragging the brush across the string on the bucket.

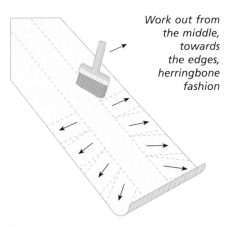

Work out from the middle, towards the edges, herringbone fashion

5 Brush the paste down the centre of the paper, then out to the edges. If any paste gets onto the table, wipe it off with a damp cloth.

GUARANTEE A CLEAN CUT

A build-up of paste on the blades stops wallpaper scissors from cutting cleanly. To avoid this, keep a bowl of water nearby and get into the habit of dipping the blades into it every time you trim the waste from a length of pasted paper. Dry the scissors before using them again.

6 Check that all the paper is evenly covered with paste, especially the edges. Holding the left-hand edge, loosely fold the paper over – paste side to paste side – to about the centre of the length.

7 Slide the paper to the left of the table so that the pasted part hangs off the edge.

8 Paste the right-hand end of the paper as you did the left, brushing in a herringbone pattern until the paper is all pasted.

9 Fold the paper over – without creasing it – so the top and bottom edges meet.

10 Leave the pasted paper to soak for as long as the manufacturer recommends. Thin paper and vinyl will be ready to hang almost immediately but heavier materials need to be left for 10 to 15 minutes.

LINING PAPER

If you are going to paper a room after lining it, make sure that the seams in the two papers won't fall in the same place.
• Start with a half-width of lining paper to stagger the joints.
• Do not overlap the edges: raised areas will show through.
• Do not take lining paper around corners. Trim away any excess paper so that the edges fit neatly.

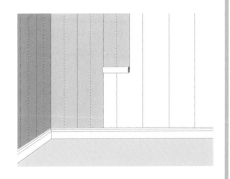

Hanging the first length

Start hanging the paper on a wall next to the window wall and work away from the light source, so that any slight overlaps will not cast shadows, which make the joins obvious. If there is more than one window in the room, treat the larger one as the main light source.

2 Hold the plumb line to the mark and let the bob hang free about 1.2m down the wall. When the bob settles, make another pencil mark directly behind the string. Check the distance to the corner all the way down the wall. If it is greater than 480mm at any point because the corner is not true, not enough paper will turn. So make the top measurement shorter, use the plumb line again and draw new pencil marks.

3 Carry the pasted length to the wall and release the top fold gently, holding it at both sides. Do not let the lower half suddenly drop – it may tear, or stretch and cause matching problems.

1 Pencil a mark near the top of the wall, 480mm out from the corner, so that enough paper will turn onto the window wall.

4 Hold the top right corner against the wall so that the right-hand edge of the paper aligns with the pencil mark. Make sure about 50mm of excess paper is left at the top of the wall for trimming.

5 Keep the left edge of the paper off the wall while you align the right-hand edge on the lower pencil mark.

6 Once the right edge is in place, smooth the paper with your hand or paperhanging brush diagonally up until the top left corner of the paper is on the wall.

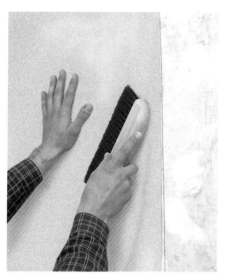

7 Let go of the paper and smooth out the top half of the length with the paper-hanging brush, working from the centre outwards. Make sure the paper stays on the pencil mark.

8 Release the lower fold. Brush down the centre of the length, then out to the edges as you did when pasting, ensuring that any bubbles are brushed out. Dab down the edges with the tip of the brush or a dry, clean cloth made into a pad.

9 With the length in place, run the back of a pair of scissors along the paper where it meets the skirting board, to crease it.

10 Pull the paper gently away from the wall and cut along the crease, with the underside of the paper facing you. Brush the trimmed edge back in place. Repeat this process at the top of the length.

Alternatively A trimming guide gives a neater edge once you have learnt how to handle it properly. Slide the guide under the paper and cut off the excess with a trimming knife. The blade must be razor-sharp or it will tear the damp wallpaper. If you feel the knife pulling at the paper, change the blade immediately.

Hanging the next lengths

1 Hang the second length of paper to the right of the piece on the wall, following the same procedure but without using the plumb line. Match the top section of the left edge of the new length with the length on the wall, then run your hand diagonally up and to the right to press the top of the paper to the wall.

2 Smooth out the paper from the centre with the paperhanging brush.

3 Release the lower fold, check that the edges match and continue to brush over the paper. Trim top and bottom as before.

4 With two or three pieces hung, run the seam roller lightly down the joins of smooth papers. Do not press down the edges of textured materials, like Anaglypta, or lines will show where the pattern has been flattened.

HELPFUL TIP

Use matchsticks to mark where fittings have been taken down from a wall. Push a matchstick into each hole or wallplug, leaving it just proud of the surface. Ease the matchsticks through the paper when you smooth it over the wall. Snap the tip off each matchstick first to prevent it from staining the paper.

HANGING WALLPAPER

Wallpapering around corners

All rooms have internal corners and often external ones as well – on a chimney breast for example.

Internal corners

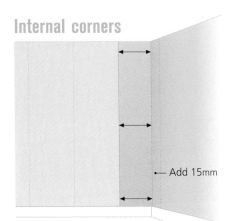

Add 15mm

1 Measure the distance between the last length you have hung and the corner at the top, middle and bottom of the wall. Note the widest distance and add 15mm to allow for the turn onto the next wall.

2 Cut a length to this width. Keep the offcut for papering the first section of the adjoining wall.

3 Paste and hang the length. Take the overlap onto the next wall. Use the brush to smooth the paper well into the corner. If creases form, tear the paper – but cut vinyl – and overlap the torn pieces so that they lie flat (see box below).

4 Measure the offcut and hang the plumb line this distance away from the corner to find a vertical. Make pencil marks behind the line at intervals down the wall.

MASKING A CREASE

Wallpaper may crease as you turn it round an out-of-square corner. If it does, tear the paper along the crease line while it's still wet, then smooth it back into place with the 'white' of the tear on the underside. The repair will be almost invisible. Don't tear vinyl: cut the creases instead. You'll need to use overlap adhesive to stick the edges down.

5 Hang the offcut with the right-hand edge aligning with the pencil marks. The length will overlap the paper turned from the previous wall. If the paper is patterned, match the two pieces as closely as possible. Use special overlap adhesive with vinyls to make the overlap stick down firmly.

External corners

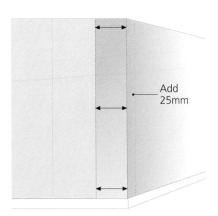

Add 25mm

Never try to turn more than 25mm around an external corner – the turned paper is likely to slant and look crooked. This technique can be applied to rounded walls as well as right-angled corners.

1 Paper the wall until there is less than one width to the corner.

2 Measure the distance between the edge of the last hung length and the corner, at the top, middle and bottom of the wall. Add 25mm to allow for the turn and cut the paper to this size.

3 Hang the length as far as the corner and take the overlap around onto the next wall. Smooth away any bubbles with the paperhanging brush.

HELPFUL TIP

Vinyl will not stick over vinyl, whether it's ready-pasted or not, so when you overlap edges at a corner, either cut through both thicknesses of covering to make a butt joint or stick the two together with special vinyl overlap adhesive.

---

4 Hang the offcut from the first length next to the paper on the wall, matching the pattern and butting the joins. You will be able to butt it to the turned edge if the corner is true. If it is not, hang it to a plumbed line so it just overlaps the turned edge, then cut through both layers (see

below), using a straight edge and a sharp trimming knife. Peel away the offcuts and finish the two edges with a seam roller.

APPLYING BORDERS

You can buy friezes and borders to match a fabric or the colours or motif of a wallpaper. You can also buy self-adhesive borders, which are a great way to brighten up a child's room.

A deep frieze at the top of a wall will make the ceiling seem lower. A 'frame' of frieze on the wall, set in about 250mm from the edge, will help to 'shrink' the long wall of a narrow hall or landing.

The frieze must go on a sound, flat surface; a heavily embossed paper is not a suitable surface.

Applying a frieze

1 For a frieze at the top of a wall, draw a straight pencil guideline; make it slightly lower than the depth of the frieze to allow for an uneven ceiling edge and apply a band of ceiling paint at the top of the wall. If the frieze is to go along the skirting and round a door, no guideline is needed.

2 Cut the frieze to length, using one piece from corner to corner.

3 Paste the frieze, fold it like a concertina and leave it for ten minutes to soak.

4 Apply it along the guideline, brushing it out well and letting out folds as you work along the length.

Peel and stick borders

Borders that are all-plastic have stronger adhesive than paper-backed vinyl. Peel off only a little of the release paper at a time, as they cannot be repositioned without damaging the paper beneath.

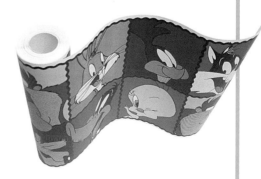

Wallpapering in awkward places

Most rooms have fixtures that are tricky to paper around. Here are some techniques that may help.

Light switches or sockets

1 Turn off the electricity at the mains. Hang the paper from the top of the wall down as far as the switch or socket.

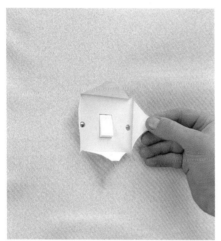

2 Cut the paper to the corners of the switch and pull back the flaps.

3 Partially unscrew the switch cover and pull it about 5mm away from the wall.

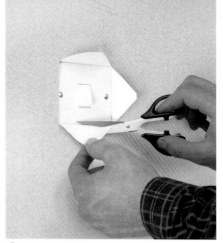

4 Trim away excess paper so that about 3mm of paper will fit behind the cover.

5 Gently ease the switch cover through the hole in the paper.

6 Push the paper behind the switch cover with a piece of flat wood, like a lolly stick, and then brush the paper flat against the wall, smoothing away any air bubbles.

7 Hang the remainder of the length. Tighten the switch cover screws and turn the electricity supply back on.

SAFETY TIP

Never put metallic or foil wall coverings behind light switches. They may conduct electricity. Always turn off the electricity at the consumer unit (fuse box) before undoing light switches or sockets.

Circular fittings

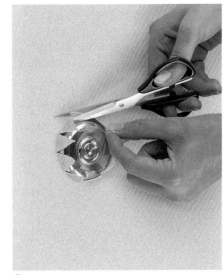

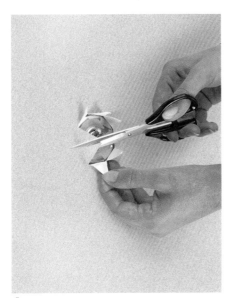

1 Hang the length of wallpaper in the ordinary way until you reach the fixture. Pierce a hole in the paper over it with a pair of small scissors. Then make star-like cuts out to the edge of the fitting so that the paper will go to the wall.

2 Crease the outline of the fitting on the paper with the back of a pair of scissors.

3 Cut off the surplus paper with small pointed scissors – they must be sharp or you may tear the wet paper. Follow the marked outline but allow for just a fraction of paper to turn onto the fitting so that the wall cannot show through a gap.

4 Smooth the paper flat around the fitting with a paperhanging brush. Then hang the rest of the length.

HELPFUL TIP

If the trimming takes some time and the paste is beginning to dry, apply a little more paste to the wall, rather than to the paper.

Radiators

1 Tuck the paper in behind the radiator until you reach the supporting bracket. Hang the next piece over the radiator, brushing it flat as far down as possible.

2 Use a pencil to mark the position of the wall bracket on the back of the paper and make a vertical cut in the paper from the bottom edge to the top of the bracket.

3 Feed the paper down behind the radiator and smooth down with a radiator roller. Trim it at the skirting board. Alternatively, if the radiator overhangs the skirting board, save paper by trimming it off 150mm below the top of the radiator.

4 Sponge any paste off the radiator before it dries.

HELPFUL TIP

When wallpapering a room with a radiator, turn off the radiator and allow it to cool completely before you start. Not only will it be more comfortable than working round a hot radiator, but your results will be better, because there will be no risk that the paper may dry too fast and start to curl.

GETTING BEHIND RADIATORS

If you are unable (or unwilling) to remove the radiators before papering a room, cut the paper to length so you can tuck about 200mm down behind them. Use a radiator paint roller if you have one to press the paper into place. Otherwise improvise by taping some sponge to a slim batten (as shown).

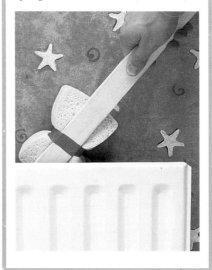

CHIMNEY BREASTS

If you have chosen a strongly patterned wallpaper, centre it on the chimney breast and hang subsequent lengths from here towards the room corners. If there is no dominant pattern, hang the wallpaper round the chimney breast in the same way as for other corners (page 70).

Fireplaces

1 Cut the lengths of paper that are to go round the fireplace roughly to size before applying paste – so that you do not have to cope with a lot of pasted paper when trimming. Leave a margin of at least 25mm for trimming in situ.

4 Smooth the paper in place all around the fireplace, using the points of bristles of a paperhanging brush to push the paper into awkward corners. Continue down to the skirting board.

Door frames

The techniques for papering around doors are similar to those used around fireplaces.

1 When you get to the door, hang a pasted full-length strip next to the last length, allowing the strip to flap over the door. Press the paper against the top corner of the architrave. Make a diagonal cut from the loose edge to the architrave top corner.

2 Brush paper into the angles between the wall and the architrave above and beside the door. Use scissors to crease the paper.

3 Trim off the excess paper along the side of the door, working from the bottom upwards. Then cut off the waste paper above the door opening.

4 Using a paperhanging brush, press the trimmed edges back into place against the edges of the architrave. Then cut the top edge of the length to fit at ceiling level, and the bottom edge at the skirting board.

5 You will probably need to hang a short length of wallpaper above the door. Use scissors to crease the paper into the angle between wall and ceiling, then into the angle between wall and architrave. Trim the paper to fit. When cutting above the architrave, leave the paper slightly long, so that it covers the top edge of the architrave.

6 Repeat steps 1 to 4 to hang another full-length strip at the opposite side of the door opening. Brush the cut edges back into place and carry on papering the rest of the wall

2 Paste and hang the paper in the ordinary way as far as you can, then mark the outline of the fireplace on the paper using the back of a scissor blade.

3 Peel a little of the paper away from the wall so you can work comfortably. Cut along the marked outline. Use small, sharp scissors if there are lots of small cuts; otherwise, use paperhanging scissors.

Recessed windows

1 When you reach a window recess, hang a full length drop of paper so that it overlaps the opening. If the overlap is large, you may need a helper to support the weight of the pasted paper.

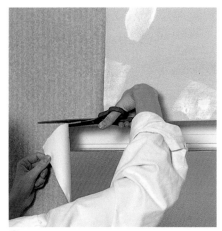

2 Make a neat, horizontal scissor cut level with the top edge of the recess.

3 Make a second cut level with the top surface of the window sill.

4 If the flap of paper that you have created is enough to cover the depth of the recess, crease it into the angle with a paperhanging brush. Run scissors along the crease to make a defined cutting line. Peel back the paper and make a neat scissor cut to trim off the excess. Brush the paper back into place.

5 If it is not deep enough to reach the window frame, cut and paste a strip a little wider than the gap and hang it on the side of the reveal, matching it to the pattern, if there is one.

6 Cut a piece of wallpaper long enough to reach from the ceiling to the top of the window, into the recess and up to the frame, with extra for trimming. Hang this next to the previous full-length strip, and brush into the recess. Trim at ceiling level and where paper meets the frame. Repeat until you need another full-length piece.

7 Paper under the windowsill. Measure from the underside of the sill to the top of the skirting board, then add 50mm or so for trimming. Cut strips of paper to this length and hang them under the window, matching the pattern if necessary. Repeat to cover the rest of the wall below the window opening, stopping when the next piece needed is a full-length one.

8 Check that the last piece hung above the window is in line with the last piece below it by hanging a plumb line. If it is not, measure the discrepancy at its widest point and subtract this from the width of a piece of paper. Mark a plumb line on the wall to the right of the window at this distance from the edge of the overhanging piece of paper.

9 Hang the next whole length. Butt it up to the previous pieces if they were in line, or, if the paper above and below the window was misaligned, position its right hand edge level with the plumb line you have drawn.

10 There will be a gap in each top corner of the reveal. Cut a strip of paper the width of the gap at top left, but 50mm deeper than the recess. Position the paper over the gap, allowing about 25mm to turn up at the front edge onto the wall above, matching the pattern, if there is one.

11 Use a trimming knife and straight-edge to cut through both the patch and the paper above it, 15mm above the edge of the recess. Peel away the offcuts from each piece and then press the edges flat for

an invisible butt join. Cover the gap in the other corner of the reveal in the same way.

1 Cut the first length that overhangs the window (at the right of the window below) so that a flap folds round to paper the reveal. 2 If the flap is not wide enough (see the left-hand side of the artwork) you will need to fill in with a patch. 3 The top corners at each side of the reveal will also need to be patched (right). 4 Hang a plumb line to check that the paper above the window is in line with that below. If it is not, hang a second line to determine a plumb left-hand edge for the next length of paper, allowing enough to fill the gap at its widest point.

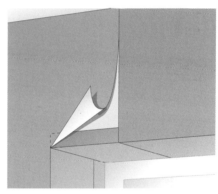

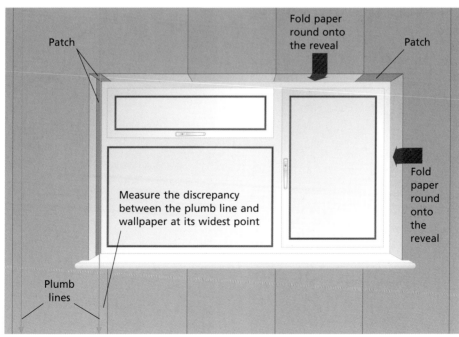

Patch

Fold paper round onto the reveal

Patch

Measure the discrepancy between the plumb line and wallpaper at its widest point

Fold paper round onto the reveal

Plumb lines

Hanging special coverings

Some wallcoverings require special techniques, such as pasting the wall instead of the paper. Other papers come ready-pasted and you don't even need a pasting table to hang them successfully.

Hanging paste-the-wall paper

This type differs from standard wallpaper because you do not cut lengths from the roll before you hang it. You also paste the wall and not the wall covering.

1 Hang a plumb line and mark a true vertical on the wall as for hanging standard wallpaper (page 68).

2 Paste the area of the wall which the first length is to cover, taking the paste just beyond the width of the covering. Use an adhesive containing a fungicide and apply it with a paint roller or brush.

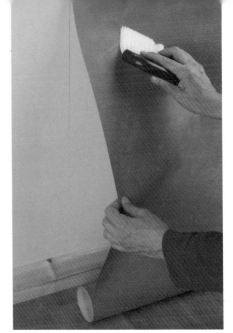

3 Hold the roll of paper up to the pasted area. Align the right edge with the pencil marks on the wall. Smooth the covering into place with a brush or damp sponge.

4 Gradually unroll the paper as you move down the wall, wiping away any bubbles under the surface as you work. You may find it easier if a helper holds the roll.

5 Crease the covering at the top and bottom of the length as for standard wallpaper and trim.

6 Paste an adjacent width of the wall and hang the next length as before. Make sure the pattern matches, and butt join the edges of the two pieces.

Hanging ready-pasted papers

Ready-pasted papers and vinyls are water-resistant so they do not expand in water. This reduces the chance of bubbles forming and they do not have to be left to soak.

Tools Water trough (cheap polystyrene troughs are widely available in DIY stores); scissors; pasting brush; sponge.

Before you start Hang a plumb line to find a true vertical and make pencil marks to act as a guide for the first length as for hanging standard wallpaper (page 68). Put down plenty of dust sheets and fill the water trough with cold water. Position it near the wall where you are going to start.

1 Measure the wall height, add 100mm for trimming and cut a length of the paper or vinyl. Check which way up it is to be hung on the wall.

2 Roll the cut length up loosely, paste side out, from bottom to top, and immerse it in the trough for the recommended time.

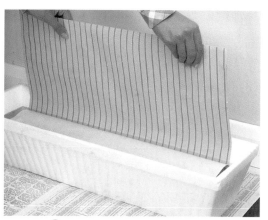

3 Use both hands to lift the covering out of the trough. Hold the length above the trough for a few seconds so that surplus water drains into it.

HELPFUL TIP

Mix a small amount of paste even when you are hanging ready-pasted papers. Use it to revive areas that may have dried out while you have been trimming. Brush the paste onto the dried areas and then smooth the length into place.

4 Hang the length, smoothing away air bubbles with a clean sponge. Work from the middle of the length out to the edges as for standard wallpaper.

5 Wipe away any excess paste at the seams with a damp rag. The paste will not stain the surface of the covering.

6 Trim the edges as you would standard wallpaper. Then cut the next length. Roll, soak and hang it following the same procedure as for the first length.

7 Keep the water trough topped up with water as you hang the lengths. Move the trough along as you work your way from one end of the wall to the other.

8 Use special overlap adhesive to get a good bond where vinyl overlaps vinyl (around corners for example) or where a seam is not lying flat.

9 Cut vinyl with scissors around awkward angles. You cannot tear it. If you have to overlap vinyl, you can make the join less noticeable by tearing off the backing paper of the top layer of vinyl, to reduce its thickness.

10 When you have hung three or four lengths, go over the seams with a seam roller to ensure that the edges are firmly stuck down.

Wallpapering a ceiling

Ceilings are hard to decorate – you have to work at a height and against gravity. Also, because the ceiling is usually well lit, any imperfections in your work will show up. If the ceiling is smooth, consider painting it rather than papering it. You may want to paper a ceiling for a decorative effect or line a ceiling that has hairline cracks before painting it.

Tools Dustsheets; tacks and chalk-line; scissors; pasting brush; wallpaper hanging brush; stepladders and trestle boards; pasting table; sponge.

Materials Paper; wallpaper paste.

Before you start Cover the floor with plenty of cotton dust sheets. Set up a safe working platform. Use two trestles or two stepladders and arrange a scaffold board between them so that the ceiling clears your head by about 75mm. If possible,

---

MANY HANDS MAKE LIGHT WORK

Papering a ceiling is much easier if you have someone to support the concertina folds of pasted paper while you line the length up and brush it into place. Make up a T-shaped support from timber off cuts (below), or use a clean soft broom.

---

the board should allow you to paper the length of the ceiling without rearranging the platform. Use two boards – one on top of the other – to give a firmer support if the trestles are more than 1.5m apart. Fill any holes and cracks and seal any stains.

Tips for a professional finish

1 Hang paper beginning at the main window and working away from it. If there are two windows in a room, hang the paper across the narrower width.

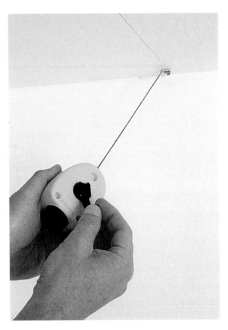

2 If you are hanging a decorative wallpaper, make a line parallel with the wall as a guide for the first length (this is not necessary for lining paper or woodchip – just align the paper with the wall). The wall is unlikely to be perfectly straight, so pin one end of the chalk line to the ceiling 25mm closer to the corner than the width of your paper. Take the line to the other side of the room, position it at the same measurement from the opposite corner and snap the chalk line to make a straight line to work from.

Hanging the paper

1 Brush the whole ceiling with glue size – this gives good slip and helps the adhesion.

2 Measure the ceiling, add a few centimetres for trimming at each end, and cut the first length.

3 Paste as for paper going on a wall but, because of the length of the paper, fold it concertina fashion as you apply the paste. Keep the width of the folds to about 450mm and do not crease the folds.

4 If you are right-handed, hold the pile of folded paper in your left hand. Stand on the right hand end of the board, facing the window. If you are left-handed, hold the paper in your right hand and begin at the other end.

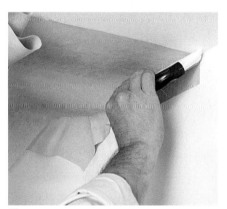

5 Release the top fold of paper. Hold it up to the ceiling and position it so that the right-hand edge aligns with the marks. Smooth the paper into the corner with your fingers. When you are satisfied that the paper is positioned correctly, gently go over it with the paperhanging brush.

6 Carefully move your left hand away to release the next fold of paper. Smooth out the paper with the brush as you move slowly to the left, checking that the paper is following the guideline. The paper will not pull away from the ceiling as long as you keep holding the rest of the paper fairly close. If the paper pulls away easily, the paste is not strong enough, so mix up some more, adding less water. Apply the paste to the ceiling, then smooth the paper back into its position.

7 When the whole length is stuck to the ceiling, trim the edges against the wall and the ends. Make a crease with the back of a pair of scissors, pull the paper slightly away from the ceiling and cut away the excess.

8 Continue to hang paper in the same way, butt joining the edges.

SAFETY TIP

If you plan to fit paper behind a ceiling rose rather than around it, turn off the electricity at the consumer unit (fuse box) before unscrewing the rose cover.

Papering around a ceiling rose

1 Hang the first part of the length as far as the ceiling rose.

2 Make a cut in from the nearest edge of the length to the point where the fitting has to go through the paper.

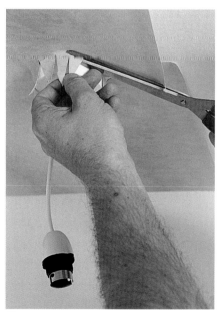

3 Make a series of star-shaped cuts to go round the fitting.

4 Hang the remainder of the length. Go back to the rose and trim away the surplus paper with small sharp scissors to make a neat fit. See page 73 for more advice on papering around circular fittings.

Wallpapering a stairwell

There are two problems that must be overcome when you paper a stairwell – how to cope with long lengths of pasted paper and how to reach all of the walls.

Hanging the paper

Until you are experienced, choose a good quality wall covering with a non-matching pattern. Matching long lengths is difficult because they tend to stretch and tear easily if the paper is thin. Hang the paper as on an ordinary wall, but take care when cutting lengths to size. Because stairs rise at an angle, each length of paper will need to be longer at its lower edge.

Papering a stairwell is much easier with two people. Long lengths of pasted paper are heavy to handle, so if possible get someone to stand on the stairs below where you are hanging the paper to hold the bulk of it while you hang the top.

Reaching the walls

You need to be able to reach both the head wall and the well wall from a safe working platform.

You may prefer to reach the walls from a staircase platform, especially if the ceiling is high, although it can be difficult to walk up and down the stairs while it is in place. You can hire a staircase platform designed for use on stairs, with a base only 610mm wide and adjustable feet.

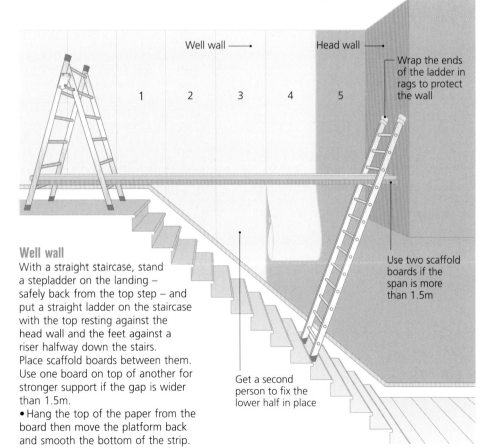

Well wall ⟶

Head wall ⟶

1   2   3   4   5

Wrap the ends of the ladder in rags to protect the wall

Well wall
With a straight staircase, stand a stepladder on the landing – safely back from the top step – and put a straight ladder on the staircase with the top resting against the head wall and the feet against a riser halfway down the stairs. Place scaffold boards between them. Use one board on top of another for stronger support if the gap is wider than 1.5m.
• Hang the top of the paper from the board then move the platform back and smooth the bottom of the strip.

Get a second person to fix the lower half in place

Use two scaffold boards if the span is more than 1.5m

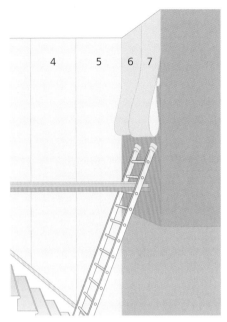

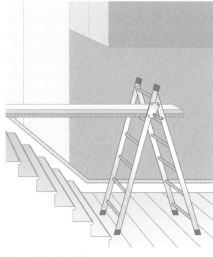

Upper head wall

Paper the upper head wall before the lower head wall.
• You will probably need two or three lengths of paper. Paste and fold them before climbing onto the platform.
• Get a helper to pass them up one at a time and hang the top of each strip.
• Let them hang there.

Lower head wall

• Remove the ladder and place one end of the scaffold board on a stair tread and the other on steps at the bottom of the stairs. Adjust the height of the board so that you can comfortably reach the lower half of the head wall to hang the bottom lengths.
• Hang the bottom of the paper from the new position.

Staircase with landing

On a staircase with a landing, you may have to support the platform over the balustrade. In this situation, the straight ladder must be supported at the bottom by a wooden batten screwed securely to one of the stairs.

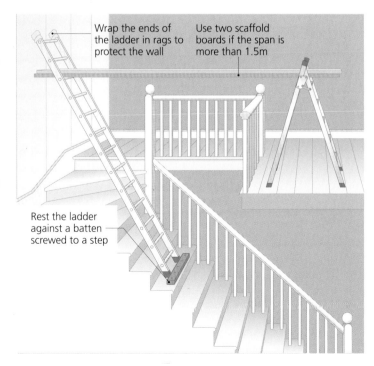

Wrap the ends of the ladder in rags to protect the wall

Use two scaffold boards if the span is more than 1.5m

Rest the ladder against a batten screwed to a step

Curing papering problems

Paper will not slide
Water in the paste is being absorbed by the wall, or the paste is drying out too quickly. Either the wall has not been sized or the paste is too watery. Make sure you mix the paste as recommended by the maker; do not add more water to make it go further.
• Put the problem paper back on the table.
• Mix a thicker paste and apply it to the wall, then re-hang the paper.
• If you suspect that the room's warmth is causing the paste to dry too quickly, open windows or turn off the heating.

Flattened relief pattern
Caused by too much pressure being applied when pressing the paper into position, particularly at the seams. Use very gentle pressure when applying relief papers, especially those that are heavily embossed. Do not use a seam roller on the edges; dab with a dry rag.

Expanded vinyls will regain their shape as the foam recovers, but nothing can be done to restore the relief pattern on others.

Shiny patches on matt wallpaper
The surface has been rubbed too vigorously when being hung. Shine marks cannot usually be removed completely, but rubbing the area with a ball of white bread may

lessen the shine. This method can also be used to clean non-washable wallpaper.

Next time, smooth matt papers carefully with a clean, dry sponge or a dry nylon or lambswool paint roller. Or dab with a rag.

Staining at the seams
Old size has been reactivated by the water in the new paste. Stains cannot be totally removed, but wiping them gently with a clean, damp rag may make them less visible. To avoid this problem, wash down walls with hot water to remove any old size, and then re-size them.

Gaps at the seams
The wallpaper might have shrunk slightly as it dried out, because the paste was not strong enough to hold it in place. Depending on the colour of the wallpaper, try painting the gap with watercolour, using a fine artist's brush, so that it is less obvious. Always use a paste suitable for the type of wallpaper being used (page 62).

Seams that lift
This often happens with vinyls and relief papers, and is caused by too little paste being applied to the edges of the paper. To re-stick the seams, lift the edge gently with the blade of a kitchen knife and apply new paste. For overlapping edges of vinyls use a special overlap adhesive.

Creases in the paper
Possibly caused by applying paper to a wall which is not perfectly flat, but more often

DEALING WITH BUBBLES
A bubble that doesn't flatten out as the paste dries is usually caused by careless pasting leaving a dry spot on the back of the paper. Make two cuts across the bubble at 90° with a sharp trimming knife or razor blade. Peel back the flaps and apply a little paste with a small paintbrush, then press the flaps back into place with your paperhanging brush.

caused by careless hanging. To avoid the problem, fill all indentations with filler or a skimming coat of plaster before papering.

Creases can be treated in the same way as bubbles. Tear the paper, or cut the vinyl, along the crease, re-paste if necessary, and smooth down.

Damp patches on wallpaper

If wet patches remain after most of the paper has dried, damp may be striking through the wall, or the patches may be condensation forming on a cold surface.

Do not ignore the problem: find the cause of the damp immediately and cure it. If treated immediately the damp patch will dry out without trace, but if left too long it will leave a stain.

Paper comes away from the wall

There are four possible causes: the paste is too weak to hold the weight of the paper; the surface has not been sized; the paper has been applied over old distemper or gloss paint; condensation has formed on the wall after it has been prepared.

If only small areas of the paper are coming away from the wall, mix a new batch of paste, apply it to the wall and press the paper back into place. If whole sheets are peeling off, strip the walls and prepare the surface thoroughly.

Brown spots showing through paper

Impurities in the plaster may be the cause, left from using a wire brush or wire wool during preparation. Alternatively, the marks may be made by mould, formed because the surface is cold and damp.

If the spots are excessive and obvious, strip the walls and prepare them thoroughly before redecorating. Treat them with a fungicide before repapering if damp is a problem. And if the wall is cold, line it with expanded polystyrene in roll form. Use a fungicide paste on condensation-prone walls, such as a bathroom or kitchen.

Repairing damaged wallpaper

Torn wallpaper can be patched using a piece of matching paper.

1 Tear off the paper from the damaged area, leaving only the paper which is firmly attached to the wall.

2 Hold a fresh piece of paper over the hole and adjust it so that the pattern matches the surrounding paper on the wall.

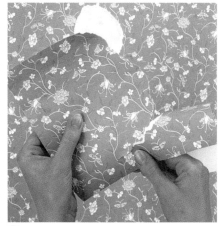

3 Tear (do not cut) a patch from the new paper so the 'feathered' edges will blend in with the surrounding paper.

4 Paste the patch and place it over the hole so that the pattern matches all round. Smooth down, working from the centre of the patch to the edges.

Patching vinyl wall covering

1 Cut a square piece of vinyl larger than the damaged area. (You cannot tear vinyl wall covering as you can paper.)

2 Tape the square over the hole and cut a square shape through both layers with a trimming knife.

3 Dry-strip the piece of old vinyl within the square.

4 Coat the patch with vinyl paste and fit it to the wall.

Tiling

Tools for tiling

Many of the simple tools required for tiling – such as pincers or pliers – may already be in your toolkit. You will also need straight battens and a plumb line to help you with positioning. The specialist tools listed here will help to make the job easier.

Sponge A small piece of synthetic sponge is a useful tool for pressing grout into the joins between tiles. However, most tubs of grout now come with a plastic squeegee that has a flexible rubber edge (see below).

Tile file Removes rough edges from a cut tile. If a cut tile is just a little bit too big, you can also file it down to the correct size.

Tile nibbler Tungsten carbide edged pincers are used for making very narrow cuts, removing waste from a curved cut or for cutting individual mosaic tiles.

Tile nibbler

Adhesive spreader and grouter A plastic tool with one notched edge for spreading tile adhesive, and the other edge fitted with a rubber blade for grouting. Small spreaders are usually supplied with tubs of adhesive. The notches on the spreader ensure that the adhesive is spread evenly.

Tile scorer

Tile snapper with scoring blade

Tile saw A tungsten-carbide coated rod, mounted in a large metal frame, which acts as a cutting blade. It is the ideal tool for shaping curved tiles to fit around obstructions, such as water pipes, wash basins or baths.

Tile cutters Cutters vary in size and shape. They are used to score a clearly defined scratch across the glaze of a tile. A cutter may resemble a slim pencil with a cutting tip or have a hardened wheel set into a handle. Some cutters have two jaws to hold the tile when you break it after it has been scored. Place the scored tile between the jaws and squeeze the handles together. For the toughest tiles, use a platform tile cutter (opposite). This can handle tiles up to 10mm thick and both scores and breaks them.

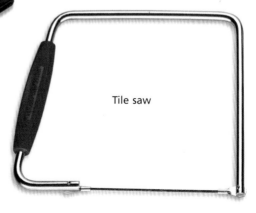

Tile saw

Platform tile cutter

Modern ceramic tiles are so hard that they are more or less impossible to cut using a traditional, hand-held cutter.
A platform tile cutter will cut both wall and floor tiles.

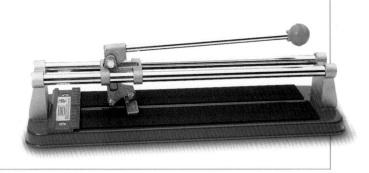

Spacers Small plastic crosses inserted at the corners of straight-edged tiles as they are applied to the wall ensure that there is an even gap between tiles.

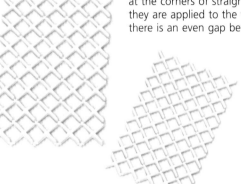

Chinagraph pencils

Chinagraph pencil and steel rule

For marking where tiles should be cut. Never use a felt-tipped pen to mark a tile – if the ink gets onto the back of the tile it may penetrate and show beneath the glazed surface.

EXPERIMENT FIRST

The cutting wheel of a pliers-type tile cutter should make a clear whispering noise when run across the glazed surface of a tile. If it makes a dull sound instead, and the tiles won't snap cleanly in the jaws of the tool, they are too hard for this type of cutter. Buy or hire a heavy-duty platform tile cutter instead (see above).

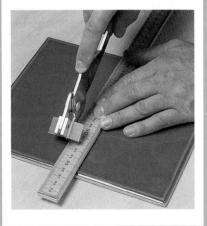

Steel rule

Tiling gauge

Tiling gauge

The gauge is a length of batten, wider than any obstruction you need to tile around. Mark the width of the tiles on the wood, plus gaps for spacers if necessary, and use the gauge to position tiles around windows or any similar breaks in the tiling.

Choosing ceramic tiles and trim

Ceramic tiles are a functional form of wall covering, particularly useful in bathrooms and kitchens. An enormous range is available in prices that vary according to size, colour and quality.

Tile sizes Wall tiles are available in sizes from 100mm square to 330 x 445mm. Some tiles are still manufactured in notional imperial sizes, typically $4\frac{1}{8}$in or 5in, giving rise to some odd metric conversions. Choosing a size that neatly fits the space you have to cover can save a lot of cutting and wastage. Remember to allow for your desired grout width when calculating how many tiles will fit your space.

HOW MANY TILES DO YOU NEED?

• Tiles are sold singly, or in boxes containing a specified number, or by the square metre.
• Before you buy or order tiles, measure the height and width of each part to be tiled and multiply the two figures to give the area in square metres. Add all the figures together to give the total area. Coverage is also stated on boxes. Allow 5 to 10 per cent extra for cutting and breakages.
• If you are going to use contrasting coloured or patterned tiles among plain ones, decide where they are to go and how many you need. This is easier if you make a plan of the wall on graph paper. Alternatively, cut pieces of paper into tile shapes and stick them to the wall to help you to get the height and spacing of the patterned tiles right. It will probably take a couple of hours, but it gives a better impression of how the tiles will look when the job is finished.
• There is always a slight colour variation between tiles. If you can, buy tiles in boxes with the same batch number. Then shuffle the tiles to disperse and hide any differences before you start to tile.

Decorative tiles Many tile ranges include decorative patterned tiles, which may have a raised or printed motif that is painted by hand or machined. They can make attractive insets in a plain tiled wall.

Imported tiles Foreign ceramics are often harder, thicker and heavier than standard ceramic tiles, so experiment on a couple of tiles to see whether you can cut and shape them before you buy in bulk. Occasionally imported tiles are glazed on one or more edges. If the tiles have plain square edges you will need to use spacers.

Insert tiles In some ranges, manufacturers supply special tiles to which bathroom accessories like towel rails, soap dishes and lavatory-paper holders are attached. Even though they are heavier than ordinary tiles, they can be fixed to the wall with standard adhesive. Check that the particular insert tile you want is available in the colour you have chosen before you buy the tiles.

Mosaic tiles Small ceramic or glass tiles, known as chips, usually 20 to 25mm square. They are supplied bonded to nylon or paper mesh or faced with paper, in sheets about 300mm square or rectangles 300 x 610mm. The mesh or paper controls the spacing between the tiles.

Borders and trims

Ceramic trims You can finish off the top edge of a half-tiled wall with a row of border tiles, or use a slim pencil bead trim in a matching or contrasting colour if you prefer. Border tiles can also be used between areas of standard tiles on a fully tiled wall, for example to create the effect of a decorative dado. Border and trim tiles are made in sizes to match standard tile widths so vertical joints will align.

Plastic and metal profile trim Strips of edging trim are available in a variety of colours and finishes, from white plastic to shiny chrome and in 2.4m lengths. A curved bead is attached at right angles to a thin perforated backing plate, which is fixed to the wall behind the last tile in each row, using tile adhesive. The tiles butt up against the edging strip, protecting their unglazed edges and creating a neat finish.

Worktop trim A neat way of edging a tiled worktop is with a timber moulding. Paint, varnish or stain the moulding first, then screw it to the edge of the worktop to help you to position the tiles and bed them to the correct level. Use epoxy grout to fill all the joints to give the worktop a hard-wearing and hygienic finish.

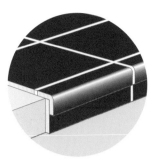

Waterproof worktops Use special angled tiles to make the edge of a homemade chipboard worktop waterproof. Stick cut tiles along the edge of the worktop first, then position the angled tiles (above) so that they overlap the face tile. Finish off by tiling the worktop from front to back, with cut tiles fitted against the wall.

EDGING A BATH OR SHOWER

When a bath or shower tray is in use, it can 'give' slightly and pull away from the bottom row of tiles around it. Flexible mastic sealant will allow for a degree of movement, but a new edging product is also available, which is designed to eliminate cracks in the sealant or grout. Bed the beaded edge into tile adhesive below the bottom row, or fix it to the face of existing tiles. Stick the adhesive sealing strip to the bath or shower tray, and it will stretch within the beaded strip as the fitting flexes.

Preparing the surface

The glaze on tiles will highlight even tiny undulations in a wall so the surface must be as flat as possible.

Plaster

Sound, bare plaster is an ideal surface for tiling. The adhesive will fill minor cracks and holes; patch larger defects with a skim of ready-mixed repair plaster then seal bare plaster with plaster primer. Scrape any loose paint from painted walls and key gloss-painted walls with coarse wet-and-dry abrasive paper.

CHOOSING TILE ADHESIVE, GROUT AND SEALANT

Tile adhesive and grout come in several forms. The most widely used is an all-in-one ready-mixed product that sticks the tiles and fills the joints, and is water and mould-resistant. It is an ideal choice for most tiling jobs. One 10 litre tub will cover an area of 10–12m².

Separate grouts and adhesives You can also buy adhesive and grout as separate products, in ready-mixed or powder form, which you mix with water. Do this only if you want to use coloured grout, or if you are tiling a kitchen worktop where a special epoxy grout is recommended for hygiene reasons. Powder products are cheaper than ready-mixed options, so may be worth considering for large tiling projects.

Sealing joints Use flexible mastic, not grout, to seal the joints between tiles and bathroom fittings or kitchen worktops (see also page 91 for a flexible beaded trim). Use mastic also to fill internal corners and the joins between tiles and skirting boards or door architraves.

Tile spacers X-shaped plastic spacers are essential for spacing tiles evenly. They come in sizes from 2 to 5mm thick. Use 2mm spacers with 100mm square tiles, and larger sizes with bigger tiles.

Plasterboard

You can tile over painted plasterboard; seal bare plasterboard with two coats of emulsion paint. Use water-resistant boards such as Aquapanel instead of ordinary plasterboard for shower cubicle walls.

Papered walls

Strip all wallcoverings before tiling, and seal bare surfaces as described above.

Worktops

Before tiling a laminated worktop, score it with a metal abrasive disc fitted to a power drill. Coarse abrasive paper or a file will also do the job but will take longer.

Tiling over old ceramic tiles

You can tile over old tiles as long as they are securely bonded to the surface behind. Remove any loose tiles and fill the recesses with repair plaster. Wash the old tiles with sugar soap to remove any grease and soap deposits. Arrange the new tiles so that the joints are not directly above those of the old ones. Then if the old grouting cracks, the new grouting won't.

Man-made boards

Seal board surfaces with wood primer or diluted PVA building adhesive. Use moisture-resistant boards for bath panels and similar uses in damp areas.

Planning the tile layout

Whether you are tiling a simple splashback or an entire wall, deciding where to start is always the first step. Because an area of tiling is made up of regular units, it always looks best if the tile pattern is centred on the wall – or in the case of a splashback, on the washbasin, sink or bath that it is complementing.

Tiling around a bath

A bath is usually sited either in a corner or in an alcove. If the bath fits exactly in an alcove, the tiling should finish in line with the front edge of the bath at the head and foot; if it is in a corner, the tiling should finish flush with the front edge and the end of the bath.

1 Start each row with a whole tile at the outer edge of the bath or alcove. Centre the tiling on the back wall.

2 Once all the whole tiles are in place, finish the rows with cut tiles in each internal corner.

Tiling a splashback

A simple splashback for a washbasin or sink usually consists of two or three rows of tiles on the wall above it. Because the tiled area is self-contained, you can complete the job using only whole tiles. There are two choices for centring the tile layout. If the basin is in an alcove, centre the tiles in the alcove, positioning cut tiles of equal width at either edge.

1 Mark the centre of the basin or sink on the wall above and draw a vertical line there. Place a whole tile at either side of the line, then add more whole tiles in a row until the tiling reaches (or extends just beyond) the edge of the basin or sink (below). Add a second or third row of tiles to complete the splashback.

2 If this layout means that tiles finish just short of the edges of the basin or sink or extend too far on either side, place the first tile astride the centre line instead (bottom). This has the effect of moving the tile row along by half the width of a tile, and may create a better-looking layout. Add extra rows of tiles to reach the required height.

Positioning tiles for a splashback

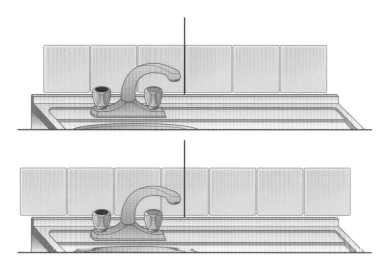

Half-tiling a wall

You can set out and centre tiles for a splashback by eye, standing tiles in a row along the back edge of the fixture to work out the best layout. On a wall, a simple aid called a tiling gauge makes the setting out much easier.

Tiling a wall to a height of about 1.2m is a popular project in a bathroom or separate WC. If the wall is unobstructed, the centring rule is simple to apply. Each row should have cut tiles of equal width at each end (except in the unlikely event that a row of whole tiles exactly fills the available space). Each column will have a whole tile at the top and a cut tile at the bottom.

You may be tempted to save work and start each column with a whole tile at floor or skirting board level, but there is a good reason why you should not do this. The floor or skirting board may not be truly level, and the effect of using it as a base-line will gradually force the tile rows and columns off square. You might get away with this on a single tiled wall, but if you are tiling all round the room the cumulative effect can be disastrous.

Using guide battens

The secret of success is to use a horizontal timber guide batten fixed to the wall beneath the bottom edge of the lowest row of whole tiles. Position it so that the gap to be filled between this row and the floor or skirting board is about three-quarters of a tile width.

You have to place all the whole tiles on the wall before you can fit any cut tiles at the ends of the rows. It is therefore a good idea to add a vertical guide batten at one side of the area, to ensure that the columns of tiles are all precisely vertical. Once all the whole tiles have been placed, remove the vertical and horizontal battens so the cut tiles can be measured, cut and fixed in place.

Using a tiling gauge

1 Measure the width of the wall to be tiled and mark the centre point. Hold the tile gauge horizontally, with one end less than a tile width from a corner, and align a joint mark with the centre line. If the gap at the end of the gauge is between one-third and two-thirds of a tile wide, you have a satisfactory tile layout. Mark the wall in line with the end of the gauge. This indicates where the vertical guide batten will be fixed.

2 If the gap is very narrow, or is almost a whole tile wide, it will be difficult to cut tiles to fit. You will get a better layout by moving the gauge along by half a tile width. Do this, then mark the wall in line with the end of the gauge to indicate where to fix the vertical guide batten.

3 Hold the gauge vertically to assess where the top of the tiled area will finish. Move it up so the bottom of the gauge is

---

MAKING A TILING GAUGE

To make it, you need a piece of 50 x 25mm planed softwood about 2m long. Choose a piece that is straight and not warped in either direction. Place it on the floor and lay a row of tiles alongside it, with tile spacers between the tiles to create uniform gaps of the correct width. Mark a pencil line on the batten to coincide with each joint. Cut the gauge to length at the last pencil mark. You can then hold the gauge against the wall to see how whole tiles will fit in the space available. A tile gauge is also invaluable for centring tiles on walls with obstacles such as windows, doors and bathroom or kitchen equipment (see page 97).

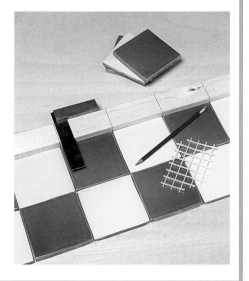

about three-quarters of a tile width above the floor or skirting board. Mark the wall at a joint mark to indicate the top of the tiled area. Make another mark level with the bottom of the gauge to indicate the level of the horizontal guide batten.

Fixing the battens

1 Fix the horizontal guide batten first, using a spirit level to get it truly horizontal. If you are tiling more than one wall, fix guide battens to each wall, and check that they are precisely aligned with each other.

2 Use a spirit level to mark a true vertical line down to the horizontal guide batten from the end mark you made on the wall with your tiling gauge.

3 Fix a vertical guide batten at this point, long enough to reach up to the top of the area to be tiled. Secure the battens with masonry nails on solid walls, and with wire nails on timber-framed partitions. Leave the nail heads projecting by about 10mm so they can be pulled out easily when it is time to remove the battens.

Fixing the tiles

With the setting-out complete and the guide battens fixed, you can start to place the whole tiles on the wall. Put down a dust sheet to catch stray blobs of adhesive, unpack your tiles and spacers and place them nearby.

Tools Notched spreader; stripping knife; damp cloth.

Materials Tiles; tile adhesive; spacers.

1 Scoop some adhesive from the tub with your spreader and spread it on the wall in a band a little more than one tile wide. The notches form ridges in the adhesive which will be compressed to an even thickness as you place the tiles.

2 Place the first tile in the angle between the guide battens. Rest its lower edge on the horizontal batten, then press it into the adhesive. Check that its edge is against the vertical batten.

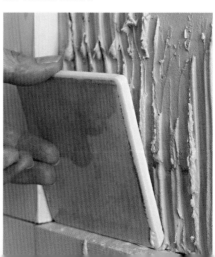

TILING

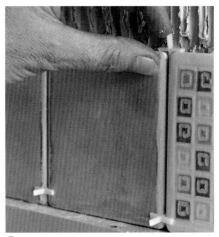

3 Place more tiles one by one along the row, fitting a spacer between them, until you reach the room corner. Press the spacers at the top corners into the adhesive so they will be covered when you fill the joints with grout (page 100). At the bottom corners, push one leg of each spacer into the gap between the tiles; these will be pulled out when the batten is removed.

4 Hold the edge of your tiling gauge across the faces of the tiles to check that they are flush with each other. Press in any that are proud of their neighbours.

5 Apply another band of adhesive and place the second row of tiles. Align the bottom edge of each one between the spacers in the row below before pressing it into place. Then fit spacers between the top corners as before.

6 When you have placed the topmost row of tiles, scrape off any excess adhesive from the wall with a stripping knife and wipe off the remaining traces with a damp cloth.

7 Allow the adhesive to set for 24 hours. Then prise out the nails that are holding the guide battens in place, taking care not to dislodge the tiles. Measure and cut individual tiles, one at a time, to fit the width of the remaining gaps (page 98) and butter some adhesive onto the back with your spreader.

8 Fit spacers into the gaps between the rows of whole tiles. Then fit the cut pieces, one at a time, into the gap between the spacers. Press the cut tile into place so its face is flush with its neighbour. Repeat the process to measure, cut and fit the remaining cut tiles at both ends of each row. Then cut tiles to fill the gap between the bottom row of whole tiles and the skirting board or floor.

Tiling around corners

Internal corners

Place all the whole tiles on both walls, then remove the guide battens so that you can cut and fit the tiles in the corners.

1 Measure and cut a tile to fit the width of the gap to be filled (page 98). Butter the back of the cut tile with adhesive and press it into place with the cut edge facing into the corner.

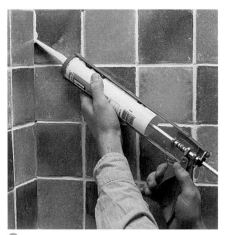

2 When the adhesive has dried, seal the angle between the two walls with a flexible waterproof mastic. This will allow for a little wall movement over time. A good tip for a neat finish is to use masking tape to mask the joint: apply the mastic, smooth it and peel off the tape once a skin has formed.

External corners

External corners should, ideally, start with whole tiles on each wall, though this is unlikely to be possible at a window rebate. Joins can be made by butting the tiles, using plastic corner trim or sticking on a strip of timber beading.

Butt joint A simple overlapping butt joint works well if the corner is true and the tiles have glazed edges. Tile the less visible wall first, placing whole tiles flush with the corner. Then tile the other wall, overlapping these tiles to conceal the edges of those on the first wall.

Plastic corner trim Coloured plastic or chrome corner trims will protect tiles on external corners from damage and give the edge a neat finish. You can use the trim along the edges of tiled door and window recesses as well.

1 Push the perforated base of the trim into the tile adhesive on one corner so that the outer edge of the rounded trim lines up perfectly with the faces of the tiles on the adjacent wall.

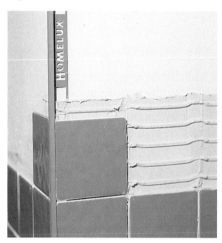

2 Start tiling the second wall, easing each tile into the corner trim as you place it. Don't push it too hard – you don't want to dislodge the trim. When you have laid all the corner tiles, make sure the trim lines up with the tile faces on both walls.

A window recess

1 Tile the wall as far as the window, cutting tiles to fit. If you have to cut a tile to an L shape, cut a line from the edge to the centre of the tile using a tile saw then score a line at right angles to the cut and snap off the unwanted piece. Use lengths of plastic edging strip designed for external corners to give the edges a neat finish.

2 Lay the tiles at the bottom of the recess first. Put any cut tiles nearest the window, with cut edges against the frame.

3 Line up the first course of tiles on the side walls with the tiles on the main wall.

POSITIONING TILES AROUND A WINDOW

Tiles look best if they are centred around a window opening. Use a tiling gauge (page 94) to span the window and adjust its position until there is an equal width of tile on either side of the opening. Mark the wall to indicate the outer edge of the tiles that will need to be cut. Drop a plumb line through the first of the lines to transfer the mark to the horizontal batten at the bottom of the wall. Work from this mark towards the corner of the room, measuring full tile widths and grout joints to determine the position of the last whole tile in each row. Fix the vertical batten at this point.

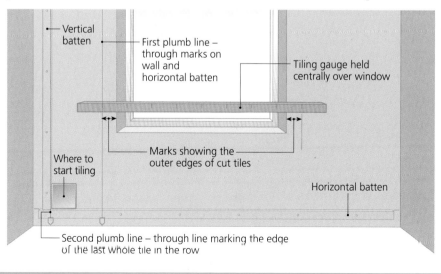

Cutting tiles to fit

It is very rare to complete a tiling job where you won't have to cut a tile. Fortunately there are a few techniques that can make cutting tiles easier.

Tools Chinagraph pencil; steel rule; platform tile cutter; tile saw; tile nibbler; pencil; G-cramp.
Materials Tiles; adhesive.

Finishing a row

1 When you reach the end of a row, place the final tile over the previous tile and butt it up to the corner. Allow for the width of a grout joint and mark the cutting line.

HELPFUL TIP

If you are filling gaps with cut tiles, butter the back of each tile with adhesive, then press it into place. It is much easier than trying to apply adhesive to a narrow strip of wall.

2 Use a platform tile cutter to make a neat straight cut. Score the tile with the cutting wheel then use the lever to snap the tile along the line. Position the tile on the wall with the cut edge into the corner.

3 Measure the final tile in each row separately. Few walls are perfectly square, so your measurements are unlikely to be the same all the way up.

Taking a sliver off a tile

1 Platform tile cutters will not make fine cuts, less than 15mm wide. Use a hand-held tile scorer and steel straightedge. Score the tile much more deeply than you would for an ordinary cut – you need to cut right through the glaze in order to get a clean break.

2 Nibble away at the sliver of tile that is being removed, using a tile nibbler. Smooth any sharp edges with a tile file.

Cutting a curved line

1 Cut a piece of paper to the size of a tile to make a template to fit around the curved object.

2 Make a series of cuts in the edge that will butt up to the obstacle. Press the tongues against the obstacle so that the creases define its outline.

3 Use the paper as a guide to transfer the curved line with a chinagraph pencil onto the glazed tile surface.

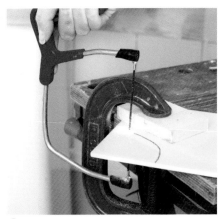

4 Clamp the tile face-up to a workbench, protecting the glaze with a board offcut sandwiched between tile and clamp. Cut along the marked line with a tile saw. Work slowly and with as little pressure as possible to avoid chipping the glaze. File away any excess if necessary to get a perfect fit.

Making holes

1 When you tile around plumbing – in a shower, for example – you may need to make holes in the tiles to allow pipes to run through. Offer up the tile from the side and from below, and mark each edge in line with the centre of the pipe. Draw straight lines to extend the marks: where they intersect is the pipe centre. Trace round an offcut of pipe – or a coin or other round object of about the same diameter – to mark a cutting line at this point.

2 Cut the tile in two along one of the lines drawn through the centre of the marked pipe hole. Score the outline of each resulting semi-circle with a pencil-type tile cutter. Use a tile nibbler to cut the hole.

POWER CUTS FOR TILES

If you have a craft drill, such as a Dremel, you can use its tile-cutting attachment to make holes in tiles. Mark the cutting line as described in step 1, but don't split the tile in two until you have made the hole. Cut out the circle you have marked then split the tile and fit it in place.

3 Fit the two cut pieces together around the pipe. Grout around the pipe or use a silicone sealant for a water-tight finish.

Grouting between tiles

When the tiles have been in place for at least 12 hours, fill the gaps between them with grout. This gives an attractive finished appearance and prevents dirt from collecting in the cracks.

Tools Pieces of sponge or a squeegee; larger sponge; thin dowel or something similar for finishing; soft dry cloth.

Materials Grout (waterproof for kitchens or bathrooms).

1 If the grout is not ready-mixed, prepare as recommended. With waterproof epoxy-based grout, mix only a little at a time – it sets hard quickly.

2 Press the grout firmly into the gaps between the tiles. Professionals use a rubber-edged squeegee, but if you have never grouted before you may find it easier to get the grout well into the cracks with a small piece of sponge.

HELPFUL TIP

Revive discoloured grout by painting it with a proprietary liquid grout whitener, applied with an artist's brush. Be aware, though, that this is a slow and tedious job.

3 Wipe away any grout that gets onto the surface of the tiles with a clean, damp sponge while the grout is still wet. Wipe away combined adhesive and grout or waterproof grout quickly – these are hard to clean off the tile surface once set.

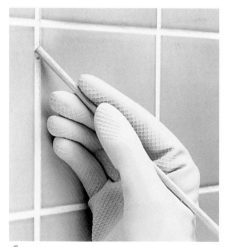

4 To give the tiling a neat professional finish, run a thin piece of dowelling over each grout line. Or use the cap of a ball-point pen, the blunt end of a pencil or a lolly stick. Wipe surplus off the surface of the tiles as you go.

5 Leave ordinary grout to dry, then polish it off using a clean, dry cloth. Another way to polish tiles effectively is to use a screwed-up ball of newspaper.

Drilling holes through tiles

Many bathroom and kitchen accessories, like soap dishes, must be screwed to the wall – in which case you may have to drill holes through ceramic tiles.

It's a good idea to make fixings in tiled walls by drilling into grout lines wherever possible, but sometimes drilling through the glaze is unavoidable. Drilling through tiles creates a lot of fine dust, which may stain nearby grouting. To catch the dust, make a simple cardboard tray and stick it to the wall with masking tape or get someone to hold a vacuum-cleaner nozzle near the drill tip as you drill the hole.

Tools Drill; small masonry bit to make pilot hole and larger one to suit the screw, or sharp spear point bit; chinagraph pencil; screwdriver; possibly steel ruler.

Materials Masking tape; wall plugs; screws.

1 Decide where you want to make the screw fixing and mark its position on the surface of the tile with a chinagraph pencil.

SCRAPE GROUT AWAY

Dried-on grout can be removed from tiles with a glass scraper. If you squeeze a little washing-up liquid along the edge of the blade, it will glide over the tile without scratching the glaze.

2 Stop the point of the masonry bit from skating over the smooth tile surface by sticking a piece of masking tape over the mark, which should show through it. Remake the mark on the surface of the tape. If you need to make more than one screw hole, use a strip of tape to cover both hole positions and mark them on the tape.

3 Make a pilot hole with the small masonry bit. Press the tip firmly against the mark on the tape. Check the drill isn't on hammer action, and start at a low speed. Drill slowly and carefully through the glazed surface of the tile. Stop drilling when the bit starts to penetrate the plaster. Using a small bit to do this minimises the risk of cracking the glaze. Repeat the process if necessary to drill a second hole through the other mark on the tape.

4 Switch to the bit that matches the screw size you intend to use. Position its tip in the hole and drill slowly and carefully through the tile and the plaster and well into the masonry.

Alternatively You can buy a special ceramic tile bit with a sharp spear point. Its shape is designed to break through the glaze immediately. This minimises the risk of skidding across or cracking the tile. The bits are available in a range of sizes.

HELPFUL TIP

If you are putting a wall plug into a tiled wall, make the hole at least 3mm deeper than the length of the plug so that it can be pushed into the wall and beyond the tile. Otherwise, when you drive in the screw, the sideways pressure within the plug may crack the tile.

Laying mosaic tiles

Mosaic tiles come in sheets with a fabric mesh backing. They are a good DIY option, being much easier to fit around obstacles than full-size ceramic tiles.

Tools Straightedge; spirit level; tape measure; pencil; notched adhesive spreader; wood batten; trimming knife; cutting board; tile-cutting pliers; grouting tools.

Materials Mosaic tiles; tile adhesive; grout.

1 Use a batten and spirit level to mark out in pencil the area you want to tile. This simple splashback is the height of a sheet of tiles above the worktop.

2 Apply tile adhesive, holding the notched spreader at an angle of 45° to create ridges of an even depth.

3 Put up the first sheet of tiles, lining it up with the guideline. Press it into place with your hand, then use a wood offcut to tamp the tiles level – especially those at the edges of the sheet.

4 When you reach an obstacle, such as a socket outlet, use a sharp trimming knife to cut out sections of whole mosaic tiles. Lay the sheet of tiles on a cutting board and run the blade along the gaps.

5 Once you have cut out the section of tiles, check the fit. There will be gaps, but you can fill these later. Spread adhesive on the wall and put the cut sheet in place.

6 Lay all the whole sheets until the area is covered. Then measure the gaps left round any obstacles. You will need to cut individual mosaic tiles to fit.

7 The best tool for cutting mosaic tiles is a pair of tile cutting pliers. Trim off a strip of tiles and score a cutting line along the whole strip. Then detach individual tiles and use the v-shaped jaws of the pliers to snap the tiles one at a time.

8 When all the tiles are in place, leave the adhesive to dry for 24 hours. Then grout the gaps between the tiles (see box opposite).

SWITCH TO A SQUEEGEE

If you've never grouted tiles, a small piece of natural sponge is the best tool to start with. Once you've gained confidence, however, a rubber squeegee does a quicker job. It is a good idea to use a squeegee when you have lots of grout joints, as with mosaic tiles or on a large expanse of bigger tiles, since it will save you a considerable amount of time. Load a rubber-edged grout spreader with grout (use waterproof grout for bathrooms or kitchens), and draw it across the tiles. Clean surplus grout off the tile surfaces as you work. Before the grout sets, use a piece of slim dowel or a proprietary grout shaper to neaten the grout lines (see page 100).

Sheets of mosaic tiles (or even pebbles) held together by mesh backing are quick to lay and flexible to use. Tiles are also available singly for intricate work or creating your own patterns.

Common tiling problems and cures

Because tiles are so hard-wearing, they are often used in areas that are damp, dirty and prone to damage. There are some common problems to look out for – treat them promptly to minimise the damage.

Mould on grout

Dark stains on grout lines may be caused by mould, which thrives in the damp and warmth of kitchens and bathrooms. Kill the mould with a proprietary fungicide, following the manufacturer's instructions. Do not use bleach. It will not destroy the roots of the mould.

Any stains left on the grout can be hidden by painting on grout whitener. When the whitener is dry, apply some more fungicide to prevent further mould.

Missing grout

If there are gaps in the grout, rake out all old grout with a proprietary grout rake (above), a small-toothed tool designed specifically for the job. Draw the rake along the grout lines, first vertically and then horizontally, to remove the old grout to a depth of about 3mm.

HELPFUL TIP

After using a grout rake on an area of tiles, use a small, stiff-bristled brush or a vacuum cleaner with a narrow nozzle attachment to remove all the debris from the joints before regrouting.

Crazed tiles

Tiles may become crazed because they are old, but new tiles may also be affected if water gets behind them. Nothing can be done to repair tiles damaged by crazing. You can paint tiles with special tile paint, though this is not as tough a finish as the original glaze. If you have spare matching tiles, you can remove the damaged ones and replace them.

Clean between the tiles

A toothbrush is the ideal tool for cleaning grout. Remove dirt and grease with a solution of liquid detergent in warm water or a non-abrasive cream cleaner. Don't use abrasive cleaners on tiled surfaces; they may dull the glaze and 'pit' the grout.

Getting into the groove

A trimming knife is good for scraping old grouting out of narrow joints, if you don't have a proper grout rake. Start at the top of the wall and take care not to chip the edges of the tiles.

• Remove surface grit by sweeping or vacuuming, then wash with non-abrasive detergent. Keep water to a minimum to prevent seepage under tiles.

Terracotta and quarry tiles
• A more rustic alternative to ceramic tiles. Quarry tiles are less porous than terracotta tiles, but do not have such subtle shading.
• Terracotta is warmer underfoot than other hard floor tiles. Hard-wearing and easily cleaned. Choice of brown and red shades.
• Noisy when walked on. Their thickness makes them difficult to cut. If laid on a timber floor, these tiles require a 13mm plywood underlay.
• Terracotta tiles need a primer or treatment before installation, plus wax or sealant every few months to maintain their finish.

Sheet vinyl
• Wide range of patterns and colours. Linoleum can be more difficult to lay but is very durable and more resistant to burns than vinyl. It comes in a range of colours and patterns.
• Hygienic, easily cleaned, resistant to spillages. Inexpensive flooring for kitchens and bathrooms.
• Smooth vinyl is slippery when wet. Cushion-backed varieties are warmer, safer and softer and quieter underfoot.
• Vacuum-clean or sweep to remove grit, which can scratch. Wash with detergent. Remove scuff marks by gently rubbing with fine steel wool lubricated with white spirit, taking care not to rub through top surface.

Carpet
• Wide range of colour and price. Available as fitted carpet or tiles. Gives feeling of

---

FINISHES FOR STRIPPED FLOORBOARDS
• Special hardwearing floor paints are available, or you can apply emulsion and then coat it with a flooring-grade varnish.
• You can give a floor an attractive 'limewashed' finish with slightly diluted emulsion paint. Apply clear varnish over it once the paint is dry.
• Rub a wax-based liming paste into bare wood with a coarse cloth and then wipe off. You can't apply varnish over wax (it will not bond or dry properly), so you will have to finish the floor with clear wax polish. This is hard work to apply and maintain, and not very durable.

warmth and comfort. Graded according to use – from heavily used stairs to low-use spare bedrooms.
• Good quality carpet is expensive. Spillages may cause permanent staining.
• Vacuum-clean frequently to remove grit which can harm fibres. Remove stains with proprietary cleaner. Rearrange carpet tiles to even out wear.

Natural fibres
• Coir, jute, seagrass and sisal flooring are all made from plant fibres.
• They come in a variety of weaves. A latex backing means the plant-fibre floor covering will not fray when cut to size, and can be laid with or without underlay.
• Durability differs: coir and sisal floor coverings tend to be more durable than seagrass and jute.
• Can stain and are vulnerable to damp – therefore they are not suitable for kitchens and bathrooms. Do not use on stairs if the finish is slippery or not hard-wearing enough.
• Vacuum-clean on a regular basis to ensure removal of grit that can harm fibres. Some types can be shampooed; others must be dry-cleaned.

Wood
• Wood floors come as strips or mosaic panels. Some are nailed down, some are glued, and some simply interlock and 'float' on the floor below. Because solid timber is expensive, most wood floors are made from laminated boards, consisting of a thin top veneer layer fixed to a strong bottom layer of softwood or high density fibreboard (HDF). For more about laminate flooring see page 115.
• Luxurious and long-lasting in living rooms, dining rooms and halls.
• Laminated boards are cheaper than natural wood, but the cheapest printed types do not wear well. Noisy underfoot.
• Remove surface dirt with vacuum cleaner to minimise scratching. Varnished floors can be wiped with a damp cloth.

Preparing a wood floor before laying a covering

Material laid on a properly prepared floor will look better and will last longer. Vinyl or cork flooring will show any ridges in the sub-floor, and will wear unevenly. Even carpet wears more quickly on the ridges.

1 Make sure that the floor is structurally sound. If it moves as you walk across it, there may be a defective joist, and you should call in a builder. If there is a feeling of sponginess, there could be an outbreak of woodworm or rot below the surface. Take up a board and check, and treat or replace as necessary.

2 Cure any damp in the floor.

3 Fix any loose boards.

4 Remove old tacks left behind from a previous covering. Prise them up with a claw hammer, pincers or tack lifter.

5 Any damaged boards will have to be replaced. If you are sanding the floor, any new boards are unlikely to match exactly the colour of the old. So replace a faulty board in a prominent place with an existing board from a less obvious spot (one that will be hidden by furniture or a rug, for example). This less conspicuous board can be replaced with a new one.

TAKING UP OLD FLOORINGS

Old tiles and parquet that are firmly stuck can form a sound base for a new floor. But carpets and sheet vinyls – and any other flooring that is not well stuck down – must be removed before you lay a new one.

A garden spade is an excellent tool for lifting a floor covering such as vinyl tiles or lino, when the glue is not holding well. Its blade has a sharp edge that you can push under the material (file it sharper if necessary) and the long handle allows plenty or leverage for lifting. For a large area, hire a powered floor-tile stripper.

Old quarry tiles are difficult to remove, and may only reveal an unsatisfactory sub-floor underneath. It is probably best to leave them in place. If a few tiles are damaged or missing, remove damaged pieces with a bolster and club hammer – wearing safety goggles. Then replace them with new tiles, or fill the gaps with sand and cement. If a quarry-tiled floor is in a very bad state, clear out badly broken and crumbling patches, clean thoroughly, fill deeper holes with sand and cement, and then apply a self-levelling compound.

Fill knots Use car body filler to block knot holes in wooden boards (left) before laying vinyl sheet flooring. If you don't, pressure from chair legs and similar objects could pierce and damage the floor covering.

Lining a wood floor with hardboard

Lining the floor with hardboard levels off boards that are curling at the edges, covers small gaps between boards and even masks minor damage.

Hardboard also covers old stains and polishes. Lay hardboard with its mesh side up. This forms a better key for adhesives than the smooth side, and when you nail down the sheets the nail heads will sink below the mesh and not create pimple marks in the final floor covering. After laying the boards, leave them at least overnight before laying the floor covering.

Tools Hammer; panel saw; large paintbrush; measuring jug; bowl or paint kettle.

Materials Sheets of hardboard 3mm thick; water; 20mm annular nails – these have ringed shafts for extra grip – about 250g for an average sized room.

1 The boards must be given a moisture content suitable for the room – a process known as conditioning. Otherwise they may become distorted. Brush half a litre of water into the mesh side of 1220mm square sheets, and stack them mesh side to mesh side, perfectly flat on the floor of the room they will occupy. Leave them for 48 hours before laying. The boards will adjust gradually to the humidity of the room, and dry out further when nailed down, tightening up like a drum skin to form a perfect surface for the final floor covering.

2 Begin laying the boards in a corner of the room, and start nailing along one edge of a sheet, 15mm in from the edge. Work

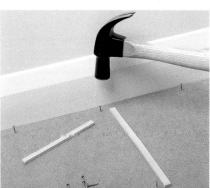

sideways and forwards, in pyramid fashion (see below). The nails should be about 150mm apart along the edges of the board and 250mm apart in the middle of the board. It helps to use cut pieces of wood as guides for spacing the nails.

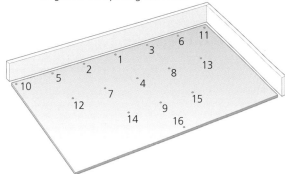

3 Butt the second board firmly against the first, and nail along the meeting edge.

4 Continue until you have to cut a board to fit at the end of the row. You do not need to cut to a perfect fit against the skirting board. Gaps up to 5mm do not matter. Use the offcut from the previous board to start the next row. This avoids waste, and prevents the joins from lining up across the room.

Restoring a wood floor

An attractive floor can be created by restoring existing floorboards. Floorboards may be stripped and varnished, or you could stain, paint or lime them before sealing with a hardwearing clear coating.

Filling holes in floorboards

Use a flexible filler to cover all nail and screw heads – nail heads should be punched below the surface, and screws may need countersinking so that their heads are below the surface. If you are painting the floor, the filler colour does not matter; if you are varnishing it, choose a filler slightly lighter in colour than the surrounding floor. Once dry, sand filler flush with the floor.

Plugging gaps between boards

There are two ways to deal with gaps between floorboards: you can fill the gaps, or you can lift and relay the entire floor.

Fill narrow gaps with flexible mastic (clear mastic will be almost invisible); wider gaps are best filled with thin lengths of square-edge moulding.

Filling gaps with moulding

1 Plane moulding strips into a slight wedge shape.

2 Apply a little woodworking adhesive before tapping a wedge into a gap, thin edge first.

RAISE THE TEMPERATURE

If all the boards in a downstairs room have to be lifted, take the chance to increase warmth by installing underfloor insulation. There are two types available. Lay nylon garden netting across the joists to support the same type of glass fibre insulation that's used in lofts. Wear gloves, safety goggles and a mask when working with this material. Draw the netting up tight before nailing down the boards, so that the blanket does not sag. Alternatively, cut rigid insulation, made from light polystyrene foam and support the slabs on battens nailed to the sides of the joists.

---

3 Plane wedges down to floor level when the adhesive has set, then stain them to match the boards.

Filling small gaps

Fill gaps between floorboards with a flexible acrylic flooring filler applied with a sealant gun. If you intend to sand and varnish the boards, use a ready-mixed tub filler that can be stained to match the board colour.

Re-laying floorboards

If you decide to re-lay the floorboards, you need to fit the first board tight to the wall, and use a tool called a floor cramp – which can be hired – to butt each board up against the previous one.

Traditional cut brads are the best nails for fixing floorboards. The length of the brads should be two-and-a-half times the thickness of the boards.

If you are laying a floor above an old ceiling, use screws, countersinking the heads, instead of nails so as not to risk cracking the ceiling beneath as you hammer.

Fixing squeaky boards

A squeaky board can be cured by driving the nails a little deeper with a nail punch. Locate the punch carefully so it doesn't skid off the nail and scar the board when you strike it. Talcum powder or chalk dust, brushed into the joints between squeaky boards, usually silences them for a while.

Sanding and varnishing a wood floor

If floorboards are sound they can be sanded to reveal a beautiful natural floor.

Sanding a floor is hard, dusty, noisy work. On fairly new boards that have not been stained or become too dirty, sanding may not be necessary. Get rid of surface dirt by scrubbing with detergent and hot water. Pay particular attention to removing dirt from nail holes.

Tools Dust mask; nail punch and claw hammer; floor sanding machine and edging sander (a weekend's hire should be enough for one room); earmuffs; sanding belts and discs (coarse, medium and fine); paint roller and wide paintbrush; fine steel wool.

Materials Flooring-grade varnish or other finish.

Before you start Punch in all the nails in the floor, otherwise they will tear the sanding belts, and remove tacks left from previous floor coverings. Remove any old polish with steel wool dipped in white spirit; otherwise the polish will clog up the sanding belt. Wear protective gloves.

1 Start at the edge of the room with your back against the wall. Keep the sander slightly away from the skirting board at the side otherwise you may damage it.

HELPFUL TIP

When a floor sander is switched on, the sanding belt starts to move, but does not come into contact with the floor until you lower the drum. Never let a moving belt touch the floor while the machine is stationary, or it will gouge a hollow in the wood. The moment the belt starts to bite into the wood – and there will be enough noise to indicate this – make sure that the machine moves forwards. It will begin to do so anyway, but an inexperienced user will tend to hold it back.

WARNING

Empty the dust bag as soon as it is about one-third full. Bulked wood dust can ignite spontaneously, especially if it is impregnated with old stain or varnish. Also empty the bag whenever you stop work for more than a few minutes.

---

2 It is normal to work along the length of the boards, as sanding across them causes scratches. But if the boards curl up at the edges, make the first runs diagonally across them with a coarse belt. Finish with medium and fine belts along the length of the boards.

3 On a floor where not very much stripping is needed, let the machine go forwards at a slow steady pace to the far end of the room, lifting up the drum as soon as you reach the skirting board.

4 If the boards are badly marked, wheel the sander backwards to your start point, lower the drum and make a second pass over the first one. Never pull the sander backwards when the drum is rotating, or the machine may pull sideways out of control and score the floor surface badly.

5 When the strip looks clean, move on to the next one, and continue to the end of the room. Raise the belt as you change direction, or it may damage the boards. You will have started each run about a metre out from the wall behind you. When you have covered the room, turn the machine round, and deal with that area.

Sanding the edges

Eventually, you will be left with a narrow border all round the room that the sander cannot reach. This must be stripped with an edging sander. Do not try to use a disc on an electric drill; it is not powerful enough.

1 Use the edging sander all round the edges of the room, taking care not to damage the paint on the skirting boards.

2 When the sanding is finished, vacuum-clean the floor to get rid of all the wood dust. Do not dampen the floor as the water may leave marks.

GETTING INTO CORNERS

You will need a sander with a pointed base to get right into corners (above). An alternative is to use a wide chisel or a plane blade to scrape the old finish off the boards. Hold the blade with bevel away from you and scrape in the direction of the grain.

3 Finally, mop the floor with a clean, dry, lint-free cloth. Be sure to shake it frequently outdoors to get rid of the last particles.

Applying varnish

The quickest way of sealing a newly stripped floor is to use a paint roller to apply the varnish. Thin the first coat as recommended on the container to aid penetration, and apply full-strength for the second and third coats. Use a power sander fitted with fine abrasive paper to sand the surface lightly between coats, and wipe it with a damp cloth to remove dust before re-coating it.

1 Apply the varnish with criss-cross passes of the roller, then finish off by running it parallel with the boards.

2 Use a paintbrush to finish the floor edges and to cut in round obstacles such as central heating pipes.

Buy a new brush
Don't risk getting specks of old paint or bristles in the varnish by using an old or cheap brush. Invest in a new, good-quality brush before you start. Synthetic fibre brushes are less prone to hair loss than natural bristle types.

Choice of varnish
Polyurethane varnish is the usual choice, but it is solvent-based and takes a long time to dry. It also tends to yellow with age. Water-based varnishes and two-part catalysed lacquers provide a clearer finish, with less tendency to discolour. They dry fast, so you can apply several coats in a day, although you have to work quickly to keep a wet edge.

Choosing laminate flooring

A laminate floor forms an overlay on an existing timber or concrete floor. Most have a wood-effect finish, but you can also buy laminates that mimic ceramic, slate or terracotta tiles, or metals such as copper or brushed aluminium. Whatever the finish, all boards are coated with tough lacquer to make them resistant to staining, scratching or fading. Special laminate flooring with a water-resistant core is made for use in kitchens and bathrooms.

Laminate flooring is made from lengths of high density fibreboard (HDF). There are locking or tongue-and-groove versions. Locking planks have tongues on their sides and ends that lock together, so you don't need to glue them. It is easy to unlock them if, for example, you want to replace a damaged board or need access to the floor beneath. Tongue-and-groove boards are glued together at each join, and so cannot be lifted easily.

The flooring is generally sold in packs. The pack will state the area it covers and whether or not the product is suitable for bathrooms and kitchens. Estimate the amount you need by multiplying the width of the room by its length, and buy about 10 per cent extra to allow for wastage.

Wood laminate
Available in distressed oak, ash, rich chestnut and many other finishes.
• Pack of 9 planks covers about 2.15m².
• Easy to install glue-free locking system.
• Can be used immediately and can be re-laid up to 6 times.
• Resistant against cigarette burns, fading.
• Cannot be used in bathrooms or other humid areas.

Synthetic stripwood
• Wood-effect surface layer (above) is a photographic copy of genuine wood grain.
• Water and stain resistant, suitable for use in bathrooms and shower rooms.
• Warm and quiet underfoot.
• Easily installed by bonding direct to a plywood or solid floor.
• Unlike real wood, the floor will not need expansion room and can be fitted up to the perimeters, making it more resistant to moisture.
• Available in pack sizes of 2.5m².

Copper-look laminate
• Pack of 7 planks covers about 1.9m².
• Easy to install glue-free locking system.
• Highly water resistant core, and so is recommended for bathrooms, kitchens and conservatories.

Bamboo
• A new flooring material (above) available in strip and finger parquet designs.
• Dark and natural light shades.
• Tongue-and-groove boards; glue together with PVA adhesive.
• Plank size: 1.2m (length) x 120mm (width) x 15mm (thickness).
• Box of 7 boards covers about 1m².
• Warm underfoot and stronger than many woods used for timber flooring.
• Environmentally friendly: bamboo is a grass and can grow up to 15m a year.

Slate-look tiles
• Pack of 5 tiles covers about 1.7m².
• Textured finish gives the impression of real slate.
• Easy to install glue-free locking system.
• Highly water resistant core, so is recommended for bathrooms, kitchens and conservatories; but not suitable for saunas or areas of very high humidity.

Laying a laminate floor

A quick way to give a room a fresh, modern makeover is to lay laminate flooring. There are two main laying systems for laminate floors: locking and tongue-and-groove.

Tools Tape measure; pencil; scissors; trimming knife; tenon saw; hand saw or jigsaw with laminate blade; hammer; tapping block or board offcut; pulling bar; power drill with flat wood bit.

Materials Enough underlay and laminate flooring to cover the room; adhesive tape; PVA woodworking adhesive; edging; threshold strip; panel pins; expansion strip (optional); fitting kit (which includes wedges or spacers and pulling bar).

Putting down an underlay

An underlay must be put down before laying any type of laminate floor. This cushions the new floor and absorbs slight irregularities in the sub-floor. If you are covering a solid floor, lay a damp-proof membrane before putting down underlay. You can buy a combined underlay and damp-proof membrane, which means fitting one layer instead of two.

1 Prepare timber floors by punching in any floorboard nails with a nail punch.

2 If you have a solid concrete floor, cover it with a layer of heavy-duty polythene sheeting to protect the laminate from any dampness within the floor.

3 Lay underlay over the whole floor, trimming to fit with scissors or a trimming knife and leaving a 10mm gap round pipes.

4 Butt joins together – do not overlap them. Secure joins with tape. If using a wood fibre underlay, allow the boards to acclimatise for 24 hours in the room before laying them, and leave an expansion gap of 5mm between the boards and 10mm round the room.

Laying locking laminate

1 Start laying the first board parallel to the longest wall in the room, in a left-hand corner, putting the end with the short tongue against the wall. Insert spacers at intervals between the skirting board and the long edge and end of the board to create an expansion gap.

2 Add more boards until you reach the end of the row, where you will probably need to cut a board.

3 If the offcut is longer than 300mm, use it to start the second row. Otherwise, cut a board in half and use that. This ensures that the joints will be staggered. Fit spacers at the end.

4 Carry on placing the boards row by row. As you finish each row, enlist help to lift the row so that the long edge is at an angle of about 30° to the previous row, and lower and push down the boards to lock the rows together.

5 At the last row you will probably have to cut the final boards down in width. Lay each board in turn over the last whole board laid, and mark the width required on it by using a pencil and a board offcut held against the skirting board to scribe the wall profile on it.

6 Redraw the line 5mm nearer the exposed edge of the board to re-create the expansion gap. Cut each board to width with a jigsaw or panel saw and fit in place.

7 Remove the spacers from the edge of the flooring and conceal the expansion gap with strips of trim to match the floor. In corners, cut the moulding at 45°, using a mitre block. Use glue or nails to fix the trim to the skirting, not to the floor.

Laying tongue-and-groove laminate

The process is largely the same as for locking laminate (left). However, because gluing does not allow for mistakes, prepare and lay two or three rows without gluing to check the fit first. Always lay boards with the tongue protruding.

6 Start the next row with the offcut from the previous row to create offset joints. Glue the grooved edge and push it into place.

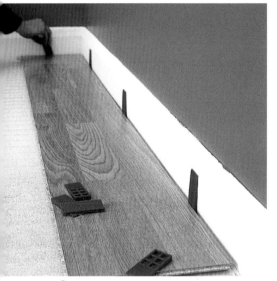

1 Lay the first board parallel to the longest wall in the room, with its groove facing the wall. Insert spacers to create a 10mm expansion gap.

2 Lay the next plank end-on to the first one, fitting the tongue into the groove.

3 When you have laid three whole rows, take them up and re-lay them using wood adhesive. Tap them together with the hammer and tapping block.

4 Wipe off any oozing adhesive straight away with a damp rag. Do this again once you have closed up the joints.

5 At the end of the row, use the pulling bar to close up the joint by hooking it over the end of the board and tapping the upstand with a hammer.

7 As you work across the room, tap the boards closely together by using a proprietary tapping block and hammer to close up the joints.

8 Follow steps 5, 6 and 7 of Laying locking laminate (opposite) to fit the last row and hide the expansion gap.

Fitting boards round pipes

the frame and cut away the wood with a tenon saw. Trim the board to shape and slot it into position. Fit a threshold bar across the door to conceal and protect the edge of the flooring. Cut the bar to the right width and glue or screw it into place.

1 To cut round a radiator pipe, align the board with its neighbour and slide it up against the pipe.

2 Mark the pipe centre on the board edge. Then remove the board, butt it up against the skirting board and mark the pipe centre on the board's short end. Join up the marks to indicate the pipe centre.

3 Use a 16mm flat wood bit to drill a hole through the board at the mark. Cut across the board and fit the two sections round the pipe.

Alternatively Almost all laminate floors come with optional accessory kits, including radiator pipe discs. These have a hole cut for the pipe: simply align the grain and glue into place to hide ragged holes.

At door openings

Cut away a small amount of the architrave and door stop to allow the board to fit beneath it. Mark the board thickness on

SOLID WOOD FLOORING

Solid wood flooring can be laid over a timber sub-floor, or directly onto floor joists if the existing timber floor is being replaced. On a timber sub-floor, the boards are laid in a similar way to laminate flooring, with an expansion gap around the perimeter of the floor area. Each board is fixed to the sub-floor using a technique known as secret nailing.

1 Drive panel pins down through the tongue of each board at an angle to the floor so it passes through the body of the strip and into the sub-floor. Use 30mm pins for boards up to 20mm thick, and 50mm pins for thicker boards.

2 Start the pins with the hammer. Use a nail punch to finish driving each pin so its head finishes flush with the top edge of the tongue. You can then slot the grooved edge of the next board over the tongue and repeat the fixing to secure it to the sub-floor.

Laying a wood mosaic floor

Full-size parquet blocks are not available for DIY laying, but wood mosaic, sometimes known as finger parquet, is an easy way to achieve a similar effect.

Tools Tape measure; chalk line; workbench; fine-toothed tenon saw; trimming knife; pencil; rag. Possibly also orbital sander or sanding block; abrasive paper (medium and fine grades); hammer; paintbrush.

Materials Wood mosaic panels; adhesive (with spreader); wood moulding or cork strip for the edges. Possibly also panel pins for wood moulding; varnish.

Before you start Wood mosaic comes in square panels about 10mm thick. They are usually backed by felt, paper or netting, but some makes are wired and glued together. The pieces are flexible, and can compensate for slight unevenness in the sub-floor. If the sub-floor is very uneven, cover it with hardboard first (pages 110–111). As wood absorbs moisture from the atmosphere, buy the mosaic panels at least two days before laying, and leave them unwrapped in the room where they are to be laid. This should prevent sudden expansion or contraction.

BUYING WOOD MOSAIC

If you can, check mosaics carefully before buying. Reject any with black marks on the face. This occurs if they are stacked with the felt backing of one against the face of the other, instead of face to face, and marks can be difficult to remove. Check, too, that the panels have been cut to the same size. Take one panel and hold all the others to it in turn, back to back. Rotate each panel through 90° for a further check of squareness. Inspect the surface for chips or scratches.

Prepacked panels usually have transparent wrapping, so you can see if the panels are face to face, and you should be able to see if they are all the same size.

1 Mosaic panels are laid in the same way as vinyl and other tiles (page 120). First set them out, unglued, to ensure the widest border of cut tiles all around the room. As with most wood floors, a border of 15mm must be left between the edge of the mosaic and the skirting board to allow for expansion.

2 Where possible, arrange the laying so that the panels can be cut between 'fingers' of wood, which only involves cutting the backing with a trimming knife.

3 When you have to cut through wood, hold the panel firmly on a workbench and use a tenon saw.

4 Use the manufacturer's recommended adhesive and spread a little at a time on the prepared floor. Lay the tiles in position, pressing them into place.

5 When you have laid the floor, cover the gap around the edges with wood moulding or fill it with strips of cork.

6 Seal the surface of the finished floor with three coats of polyurethane floor sealer, thinning the first coat with 10 per cent white spirit. Sand the floor lightly between each coat and wipe off any dust with a rag dampened with white spirit.

HOW TO REPAIR A DAMAGED MOSAIC FLOOR

If a wood mosaic floor is damaged, repair it by replacing a complete square of strips. It is a good idea to keep any panels left over from the original laying for future repairs.

1 If possible, cut around the damaged square with a trimming knife. Cut right through the felt or paper backing.

2 Lever out the damaged square, strip by strip, using an old chisel. Be careful not to damage the adjoining piece.

3 Scrape off the old backing and adhesive from the sub-floor.

4 Cut a new square from a spare panel, together with its backing, and glue it in place.

Setting out floor tiles

Lay floor tiles 'dry' from the centre of the room before you start to stick them in place, so you can achieve the best layout.

Where to start laying

Finding the centre point
Whatever type of tile you are laying, you always begin in the middle of the room, so you need to find the centre point.

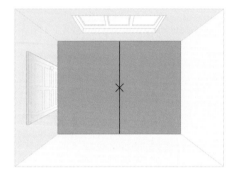

1 Measure two opposite walls and mark their centres. Snap a chalk line between these points (see box, right).

2 Measure the line and mark its centre. That is the middle of the room.

Alternatively
• If the room has a chimney breast, snap the chalk line parallel to that wall.
• If the room also has a bay, square it off with a line between the ends of the bay and measure along this false wall line.
• If the room is even more irregular in shape, choose one wall as the base wall. Snap a chalk line parallel to it, about 75mm away, and mark its centre point. Draw a short chalk line at right angles to this base line. To obtain the right angle, use a few tiles as a guide. Extend this line the full length of the room by snapping a chalk line. Measure this line and mark the centre.

SNAPPING A CHALK LINE

For many jobs, you need a line across the room. Rub chalk along a length of string or buy a chalk-line reel which chalks the string for you. Tie one end to a nail in the floor and hold the other end at the far side of the room, pulling it taut. Pull the string straight up and let go. It will mark a straight line on the floor as it snaps back into place.

Marking the cross-line

Once the main chalk line has been laid, a second line needs to be drawn across it at right angles. To do this, place two tiles on the floor, each with one side along the centre line and one corner on the centre point. Then snap a chalk line across the room, passing through the centre point and following the edge of the tiles.

Placing the key tile

You must now decide the position of the first (or key) tile, which will determine the position of all other tiles in the room.

Ideally, all the tiles around the edge of the room should be equal in size, and at least a half tile width. Experiment by laying tiles from the centre to all edges of the room.

The key tile can be placed in any of several positions:

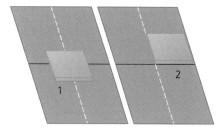

• Centrally on the middle point of the room (1).
• In an angle formed by the two chalk lines (2).

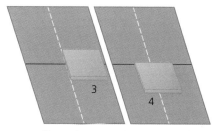

• Centrally on the main chalk line, and on one side of the line that crosses it (3).
• Centrally on the crossing line, and on one side of the main one (4).

Centring the tiles on a feature

• Some rooms have a dominant feature such as a fireplace, or bay window. To obtain an attractive result, adjust the appropriate base line – keeping it parallel to the original line – to ensure that the tiles are centred on the feature. Once again, ensure that you get the biggest possible cut tiles at the edges.
• A room may have two features. If this is the case, adjust both base lines so that the tiles can be centred on both features.
• It is not possible to centre tiles on more than two features, except by accident.

Patterns in tiles

Design your own floor patterns by combining tiles of different colours. The simplest is the 'chessboard', alternating tiles in two colours, but many other arrangements are possible.

Laying vinyl and cork tiles

Tiles take longer to lay than sheet material, but they are easier to handle and cut to fit, there is less wastage, and, if you make a mistake, ruining one tile is not nearly as serious as damaging a large sheet.

Vinyl and cork tiles are both laid in the same way. Some are self-adhesive.

Tools Tape measure; chalk line; adhesive spreader; rag; pencil; trimming knife; scrap hardboard; metal straightedge.

Materials Tiles; adhesive recommended by tile manufacturer (if tiles are not self-adhesive); perhaps white spirit.

1 Decide on the best arrangement (see Where to start laying, page 120).

2 Dust the floor and stick down the first tile, spreading adhesive on the floor.

3 Place the first tile at the start point and roll it down flat.

4 With the first tile stuck down, add adjacent tiles to form a square of four. Then work outwards from it to the walls. Where adhesive has to be spread on the floor, spread a square metre at a time.

5 If any adhesive oozes up through the joins, wipe it up immediately, using a cloth damped with water or white spirit depending on the adhesive.

Cutting border tiles to fit

The cut tiles around the edge can be dealt with in two ways. Use method 1 if adhesive is being used, and method 2 in small areas such as WCs and narrow corridors.

Method 1
Lay all the tiles except for a border of one whole tile and one part tile all the way round the room.

1 Place the tile to be cut against the last one in the row, and place another tile on top of it, pressed against the wall.

2 Draw a pencil line across the face of the tile to be cut. With some tiles you do not need to draw a line; score with a knife then snap. If the tile will not break, cut it on a piece of scrap board.

3 The two tiles now change places so the part tile lies against the wall. Put them to one side and prepare the whole row (numbering them on the back as you go), then stick them all at once.

Method 2

With this method, you lay all the whole tiles, then deal with the border of part tiles.

1 Place the tile to be cut squarely on the last tile in the row. Put a third on top, pressed against the wall.

2 Draw a pencil line across the face of the tile to be cut. With some vinyl and cork tiles you do not even need to draw a line; use a knife instead of a pencil, then snap the tile in two. If the tile will not break, cut it on a piece of scrap hardboard, using a metal straightedge as a guide.

3 The part of the cut tile closer to the centre of the room will fit the empty space perfectly. Prepare the whole row, then slot them into place.

In doorways Around a doorway architrave, you will have to draw three or four lines to create the correct pattern.

Corner tiles Tiles in corners will have to be cut to length as well as width, using the same method.

FIRE HAZARD WITH ADHESIVES

Solvent-based adhesives are highly flammable. When laying a floor with this type of adhesive, open all the windows and doors in the room and switch off any pilot lights in the room, including those in a gas cooker, gas fire or central-heating boiler. Don't smoke while you work. When you have finished, hang your working clothes outdoors to air.

Water-based adhesives are not flammable, but they take longer to dry, which slows a job down in cold weather.

Cutting round a curve

You may have to cut round an irregular shaped object such as a WC or washbasin.

1 Take a sheet of paper a bit larger than a tile. Place it over the area the cut tile will occupy, and fold it along the edges of the adjacent tiles. Tear out the corner to fit the obstacle approximately, and crease the paper firmly against its outline.

2 Cut the paper along the folds to create the template. Use it to mark the tile for cutting.

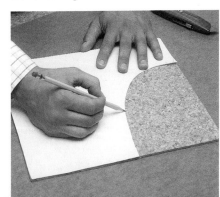

Cutting round a pipe

A pipe rising from the floor will normally be at the edge of a room, so first cut a tile to fit the border.

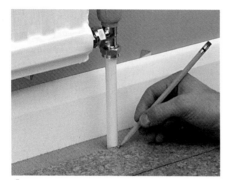

1 Place the cut tile square on the last whole tile and push it against the pipe. Make a pencil mark where it touches.

2 Put the cut tile against the wall and push its end against the pipe. Make another mark where it touches.

3 With a try square, draw a line across the tile from the mark on the side. Then put the try square on the uncut long edge and draw a line through the other mark. (Do not put the try square on the cut edge as it may not be square.)

4 Where the lines cross is the centre of the pipe. Drill a hole the right diameter (with the tile on a piece of scrap wood), or draw round a coin of the appropriate size, and cut with a knife. Cut a slit from the hole to the edge of the vinyl or cork so you can fit it round the pipe.

Alternatively You can make a very accurate hole by punching through the vinyl with a pipe offcut the same diameter. Use a round file on the inside of the pipe to sharpen the cutting edge, then strike the other end with a hammer.

HOW TO LIFT A DAMAGED VINYL TILE

To remove a damaged vinyl tile without disturbing the rest of the floor, put a piece of aluminium kitchen foil over it and press with a hot iron. Wait until the heat penetrates the tile (this will take longer on concrete than wood), then lever up a corner with a filling knife or wallpaper stripper, and pull the tile away. Lift the remaining adhesive with a filling knife heated with a hot-air gun. A larger area can be softened with a hot-air gun. The technique will not work on cork tiles, which insulate too effectively against the heat.

Lay a new tile with fresh adhesive. Do not slide it into place, or adhesive may be forced up at the edges.

Acknowledgments

All images in this book are copyright of the Reader's Digest Association Limited, with the exception of those in the following list.

The position of photographs and illustrations on each page is indicated by letters after the page number:
T = Top; **B** = Bottom; **L** = Left; **R** = Right; **C** = Centre

20 **TR** GE Fabbri Limited
   BL GE Fabbri Limited
32 **L** GE Fabbri Limited
80 **R** GE Fabbri Limited
81 **TL** GE Fabbri Limited
   R GE Fabbri Limited
   BL GE Fabbri Limited
102 **TR** GE Fabbri Limited
   BL GE Fabbri Limited
   BR GE Fabbri Limited
105 **TR** GE Fabbri Limited

   BL GE Fabbri Limited
   BR GE Fabbri Limited
108 **T** Fired Earth
109 Elizabeth Whiting & Associates/Dennis Stone
115 **T** Witex/Floorbrand Ltd
   BR Elizabeth Whiting & Associates/David Giles
116 GE Fabbri Limited
117 **TL** GE Fabbri Limited
   TR GE Fabbri Limited
   BL GE Fabbri Limited
   BR GE Fabbri Limited

Reader's Digest Home Decorating Manual is based on material in *Reader's Digest DIY Manual* and *1,001 DIY Hints and Tips*, both published by The Reader's Digest Association Limited, London

First Edition Copyright © 2006
The Reader's Digest Association Limited,
11 Westferry Circus, Canary Wharf,
London E14 4HE
www.readersdigest.co.uk

Editor Alison Candlin

Art Editor Kate Harris

Assistant Editor Celia Coyne

Editorial Consultant Mike Lawrence

Proofreader Ron Pankhurst

Indexer Marie Lorimer

Reader's Digest General Books

Editorial Director Julian Browne

Art Director Nick Clark

Managing Editor Alastair Holmes

Head of Book Development Sarah Bloxham

Picture Resource Manager Martin Smith

Pre-press Account Manager Sandra Fuller

Senior Production Controller Deborah Trott

Product Production Manager Claudette Bramble

The Reader's Digest Association Limited would like to thank the following organisations for the loan of tools, props and other materials for photographic shoots: Draper tools (www.drapertools.com); Rogers Ceramics

Origination Colour Systems Limited, London
Printing and binding Everbest Printing Co. Ltd, China

The contents of this book are believed to be accurate at the time of printing. However the publisher accepts no responsibility or liability for any work carried out in the absence of professional advice.

We are committed to both the quality of our products and the service we provide to our customers. We value your comments, so please feel free to contact us on 08705 113366, or via our website at www.readersdigest.co.uk

If you have any comments about the content of our books, email us at gbeditorial@readersdigest.co.uk

ISBN-13: 978 0276 44186 8
ISBN-10: 0 276 44186 9
BOOK CODE: 400-286-01
ORACLE CODE: 250003454H.00.24